Twayne's United States Authors Series

EDITOR OF THIS VOLUME

Warren French

Indiana University

Justice William O. Douglas

JUSTICE WILLIAM O. DOUGLAS

By JAMES C. DURAM
Wichita State University

TWAYNE PUBLISHERS
A DIVISION OF G. K. HALL & CO., BOSTON

Copyright © 1981 by G. K. Hall Co.

Published in 1981 by Twayne Publishers,
A Division of G. K. Hall & Co.
All Rights Reserved

Printed on permanent/durable acid-free paper and bound
in the United States of America

First Printing

Library of Congress Cataloging in Publication Data

Duram, James C., 1939-
Justice William O. Douglas.

(Twayne's United States authors series; TUSAS 405)
Bibliography: p. 150-55
Includes index.
1. Douglas, William O. (William Orville), 1898–1980.
2. Judges—United States—Biography.
I. Title. II. Series.
KF8745.D6D87   347.73'2634 [B]   81–2926
ISBN 0-8057-7334-7   347.3073534 [B]   AACR2

To my true friends, Erich, Bert, Zita, Zita-Ann, and Kory

Contents

About the Author

James C. Duram is a Professor of History at Wichita State University, where he specializes in United States Legal and Constitutional History. He received the B.A. and M.A. degrees from Western Michigan University. In 1968 he received the Ph.D. degree in history from Wayne State University.

He has been the recipient of several research awards and fellowships including the Henry Rowe Schoolcraft Research Grant awarded by the Historical Society of Michigan. In the summer of 1970 he was awarded a National Endowment for the Humanities Younger Humanist stipend for research in Europe on Norman Thomas's connections with European Social Democrats. He spent the summer of 1972 as a Fulbright scholar at the International Institute for Social History in Amsterdam. In 1978 he was given the Edgar Langsdorf Award for Excellence in Writing by the Kansas State Historical Society.

Professor Duram has published three books: *Norman Thomas* (TUSAS), *Soldier of the Cross: The Civil War Diary and Correspondence of Rev. Andrew Jackson Hartsock*, and *A Moderate Among Extremists: Dwight D. Eisenhower and the School Desegregation Crisis*. His articles have appeared in *Labor History, Agricultural History, Michigan History, Social Science, Kansas History, Indiana Social Studies Quarterly, Journal of Presbyterian History, Russell: The Journal of the Bertrand Russell Archives, Western Pennsylvania Historical Magazine, Missouri Historical Society Bulletin*, and *Presidential Studies Quarterly*. He has presented many papers at international, regional, and state historical conferences.

Preface

William Orville Douglas (1898–1980) symbolized different things to different people in his long, illustrious career. In more recent years, he was best known as the oft-married, crusty old liberal justice of the United States Supreme Court who practiced his own unique brand of judicial activism and civil libertarianism. During that same period, people knew him as one who spoke out frequently and bluntly on contemporary issues until a stroke forced his retirement from the bench in 1975. Others, however, know him best for his longtime advocacy of wilderness preservation, conservation, and ecology. Still others remember him as a globetrotting traveler–adventurer to places far removed and little known to most Americans. Others remember that he used his observations about life in these countries to criticize sharply postwar American foreign policy. A lesser number might recall him as the dynamic young law professor, the expert on corporate reorganization and bankruptcy, whom President Franklin D. Roosevelt appointed to head the Securities and Exchange Commission, groomed as a possible vice-presidential candidate, and appointed to the United States Supreme Court in 1939. Throughout his long public career, Douglas was never far from controversy, in part, at least, because he was never one to run away from it.

Each of the above perspectives on Douglas owes much to his extensive writings on one or another of his major areas of interest. They underscore the close connection between his own experience and his writing. Taken collectively, Douglas's writing is one of the fullest expositions of the thoughts, interests, and values of a prominent American liberal in this century. Despite its variety of subject matter, it underscores the importance of several of his fundamental beliefs and assumptions, many of which appear early in his career and persist throughout.

There is a certain amount of obvious danger involved in an attempt to characterize and assess the writings of a person whose career and activities have been characterized as something beyond capture in a verbal framework.[1] In this instance, what may be said about Douglas's career may also be said about his literary efforts. What follows, then, is not an attempt in so brief a volume to do the impossible. Because of the restrictions of size imposed on the authors in this series, the emphasis must necessarily be on an examination of the essential aspects of his writings as they appear in his most significant works.

The goals of this work are simple: it seeks to answer four questions about William O. Douglas the author. First, what major influences shaped his writings? Second, what major subjects and themes did he develop? Third, what major literary techniques did he use to achieve his goals? Finally, what can be said about Douglas's place in the American literary tradition? The answers presented to such questions in this work are not intended to provide the reader with a convenient means of avoiding firsthand exposure to Douglas's thought. They are, rather, intended to provide a useful introduction to the genuine powers of description, enthusiasm, passionate advocacy of ideas, candor, and often compelling style that have combined to make Douglas's contribution important in several aspects to the American literary tradition.

A final point is in order. Douglas's determined advocacy of his fundamental beliefs over such a long period of time spilled over into all aspects of his writing. Though a tribute to his persistence, it demands some repetition in dealing with his important ideas. It is this author's hope that the reader will tolerate such instances as evidence of Douglas's consistency.

JAMES C. DURAM

Wichita State University
Wichita, Kansas

Acknowledgments

Sitting in a small trailer in a cool, shaded glen behind a Lake Michigan sand dune, I turn to the pleasant obligation of expressing my thanks to those who assisted me in the preparation of this volume. With lingering memories of last evening's beautiful Lake Michigan sunset, with its orange, blue, yellow, gold, and, finally, pink ribbons of light among the gathering clouds, I pay tribute to the subject of this book whose writings rekindled my interest in the wonders of nature.

Special thanks go to Mrs. Connie Work, who generously made her Lake Michigan beach cottage and trailer available to my family and me during the summer of 1979 as I struggled toward the completion of this project. The little trailer in the woods provided me with a quiet place to sort out my thoughts and commit some of them to paper. I can think of no better place where I would prefer to be while writing.

A number of others greatly assisted my research efforts during the critical information-gathering stage of this project. Dean Lloyd M. Benningfield and the Wichita State University Faculty Research Committee he chairs provided greatly needed financial support. The reference staff of our university library—especially Thoburn Taggart, Jr., Russell E. Dybdahl, Dale R. Schrag, Kenneth C. Knight, and Mina Jean Waddell—provided their usual excellent support. In addition, I received invaluable assistance in locating materials about William O. Douglas from the staffs of the Hoover, Roosevelt, Eisenhower, Kennedy, and Johnson Presidential Libraries as well as that of the Oral History Project at Columbia University.

Several of my colleagues in the History Department—especially William E. Unrau, James Gray, George W. Collins, Phillip D. Thomas, Donald M. Douglas, John E. Dreifort, John L. Harnsberger, and the late Randall O. Hudson—assisted me with their discussions and criticisms of this project. So also did John E. Stanga, Jr., and Harry L. Kennedy, colleagues from the Political Science and Journalism Departments, respectively, who shared their perspectives on Douglas with me. Borrowing an expression from

Douglas, my association with all of them has left me with "a full heart."

Special thanks go to David K. Henderson, one of my Constitutional History students, for his research efforts on Douglas's legal writings. His diligence and analytical prowess suggest a great future for him.

Most importantly, I wish to express my deep gratitude to my wife, Eleanor, whose research assistance and typing skills proved invaluable. Her suggestion that we forego the heat of a Kansas summer and find a cool, secluded spot where I could write while she cared for our two children proved to be excellent advice. She and my children deserve special thanks for their tolerance of my behavior and temperament as I struggled with the manuscript for this book. All, fortunately, had been through that experience before.

Finally, despite the temptation to write them off as products of the distractions of a Michigan summer, the author assumes responsibility for any errors that have inadvertently slipped into type.

Chronology

1898   William Orville Douglas born in Maine, Minnesota, October 16; the second of three children of the Reverend William and Julia Bickford (Fisk) Douglas.

1901   Is stricken with polio, which is almost fatal.

1904   His father dies and the impoverished family settles in Yakima, Washington.

1916   Graduates from Yakima High School as valedictorian.

1920   Graduates Phi Beta Kappa from Whitman College (Walla Walla, Washington) and starts teaching English and Latin in Yakima High School.

1922   Arrives in New York City with six cents in his pocket and enters Columbia University Law School.

1923   Marries Mildred Riddle, August 16; eventually has a son, daughter, and six grandchildren.

1925   Graduates second in his class from Columbia. Starts working for a Wall Street law firm and teaches at Columbia on the side.

1926   Is admitted to the New York Bar and briefly works for a Yakima law firm.

1927   Starts teaching full time at Columbia.

1928   Accepts a position at Yale University.

1929–
1932   Collaborates with the United States Department of Commerce in bankruptcy studies.

1930–
1932   Serves with the National Commission on Law Observance and Enforcement.

1932   Accepts the Sterling Chair of Commercial and Corporate Law at Yale.

1934   Accepts a position with the Securities and Exchange Commission.

1936   Is appointed commissioner of the SEC.

1937   Is appointed chairman of the SEC.

1939   Is appointed to the United States Supreme Court by President Franklin D. Roosevelt, and eventually becomes its longest-sitting justice and one of its greatest civil libertarians.

1940   Is seriously considered by President Roosevelt as vice-presidential nominee.

1944   President Roosevelt proposes his and Harry S. Truman's names for the vice-presidential nomination.

1948   Refuses President Truman's invitation to run for vice-president.

1949   Takes first of many trips to Asia and Middle East. Is nearly killed falling off a horse when it rolls over on him.

1950   *Of Men and Mountains.*

1951   Urges United States recognition of Red China and is threatened with impeachment. *Strange Lands and Friendly People.*

1952   Expresses no interest in Democratic presidential nomination. *Beyond the High Himalayas.*

1953   Divorces Mildred. *North from Malaya: Adventure on Five Fronts.*

1954   Marries Mercedes Hester Davidson. Successfully protests a proposed highway alongside the Chesapeake and Ohio Canal by taking a 185-mile hike. *An Almanac of Liberty.*

1956   *Russian Journey* and *We the Judges: Studies in American and Indian Constitutional Law from Marshall to Mukherjea.*

1958   *The Right of the People* and *West of the Indus.*

1960   *America Challenged* and *My Wilderness: The Pacific West.*

1961   *My Wilderness: East by Katahdin.*

1962   *Democracy's Manifesto* and *Freedom of the Mind.*

1963   Divorces Mercedes and marries Joan Carol Martin. *Mr. Lincoln and the Negroes: The Long Road to Equality* and *The Anatomy of Liberty: The Rights of Man Without Force.*

1965   *A Wilderness Bill of Rights.*

1966   Divorces Joan and marries Cathleen Heffernan. *The Bible and the Schools.*

1967   *Farewell to Texas: A Vanishing Wilderness.*

1968   Has pacemaker installed. *Towards a Global Federalism.*

1970   Gerald Ford and other conservative representatives threaten him with impeachment. *Points of Rebellion.*

1971   *Holocaust or Hemispheric Co-op: Cross Currents in Latin America* and *International Dissent: Six Steps Toward World Peace.*

1972   *The Three Hundred Year War: A Chronicle of Ecological Disaster.*

1974   Suffers stroke, December 31. *Go East, Young Man: The Early Years.*

1975   Retires from the Supreme Court, November 12.

1977   Attends dedication ceremonies for the Chesapeake and Ohio National Historical Park.

1980   Dies at Walter Reed Army Medical Center, Bethesda, Maryland, January 19 at age of eighty-one. His final book, *The Court Years, 1939-1975: The Autobiography of William O. Douglas*, posthumously published.

CHAPTER 1

The Writer Emerges

I *The Shaping of an Active Mind*

WILLIAM Orville Douglas was not born to wealth or power. His rise to prominence in American society was largely the result of his own perseverance, ability, ambition, and hard work. His life experiences contain many of the classic elements of the American success epic. An examination of the details of his incredibly varied, full life explains much about the major influences that shaped his extensive writings on his chosen profession of law and his numerous avocations.

Few writers in the American liberal tradition reflect a closer connection between their life experiences and the content of their writing. The humane, liberal philosophy that dominates and transcends all aspects of his subject matter over more than a forty-year span can best be understood as the direct result of those same experiences that shaped his writings. It is because of this close connection, the ever-present autobiographical element, that this first chapter is devoted to an examination of those influences that proved to be of crucial importance in the shaping of his literary efforts as he rose to national prominence in the 1920s and 1930s. It is not a definitive biographical statement. That would be a needless repetition of facts already too well known and recorded many times before.

Despite the controversy that has marked his career and the writings of those who have assessed various aspects of it, there is agreement on one point about him. Both Douglas and critics agree that many of the influences shaping his fundamental attitudes and thus his writing were deeply rooted in the experiences of his early years.[1] It is possible to argue that the agreement on this point among those writing about Douglas since the appearance of his autobiographical works has been swept into the vortex of his

17

extremely appealing descriptions of his own life. This, however, does not explain the unanimity on that point found among those who wrote about him prior to the publication of his autobiographical works. Because of that and a continuing close connection between Douglas's experiences and the major themes in his writings, this is a critically important point. It does not mean that he emerged whole cloth from his childhood and youth with a rigidly defined set of principles that prevented subsequent intellectual development. Rather, Douglas's early experiences left him with an attitude toward life and a set of operational values and ideals that, in view of his subsequent success, later events seemed to confirm.

Nowhere are the importance of Douglas's early experiences on his later career more clearly explained than in his first two autobiographical works. *Of Men and Mountains* (1950) contains the story of his younger years and the reminiscences of his wilderness experiences.[2] *Go East, Young Man: The Early Years* (1974), the first volume of a two-volume work, repeats in an abbreviated form the earlier aspects of his life that he cited in *Of Men and Mountains* and carries the story up to his appointment to the United States Supreme Court in 1939.[3]

Though the two books were published some twenty-five years apart, they reflect thematic unity and the persistence of certain fundamental values in Douglas's thought. Of the two works, though chronologically less complete, *Of Men and Mountains* is the most impressive, because of its unity of theme, freshness of viewpoint, superb anecdotal style, and its detailed examination of what Douglas regarded as the most important influences shaping his life. Because of the seminal place it occupies in his writing on the relationship between wilderness experiences and his values, detailed analysis of the work appears in a later chapter.

An introductory generalization about *Of Men and Mountains* is in order at this point, though. It is a more pure, optimistic statement of his idealism than *Go East, Young Man*. Absent from it are the signs of the decay of this faith in the face of disillusionment that appear in *Go East, Young Man*.[4] In the earlier work, though the younger Douglas is preoccupied with the challenges facing the American people, he is less impressed with the immensity of these challenges and more certain of the people's willingness to make the sacrifices necessary to overcome them.

Go East, Young Man, as extensive passages in its early chapters indicate, is an expanded, updated version of *Of Men and Moun-*

tains.[5] Although it is his first volume devoted to personal experiences in over a decade, it is marked by the same superb anecdotal style and genuine descriptive powers that characterized his earlier works. To say this, however, is not to deny its worth. Douglas has succeeded in applying the "feeling intellect" to recreate with clarity the seminal events of his earlier life.[6] Those who have read extensively in his writings will detect in this volume a more purposive effort to describe the influences that shaped his controversial judicial philosophy. Those who have not will find it a good starting point for understanding that critical aspect of his literary personality.

If the worth of an autobiography is determined by what it reveals about the man who writes it, this work, with the possible exception of the author's treatment of his relationship with his first wife, must be judged a success. One can see very clearly the effects of his successful struggles against polio, an overprotective mother, the dangers of the wilderness, the temptation to settle for a lucrative corporate practice, and the pitfalls of too much ambition. Douglas's explanation of the role that the *O'Malley* case played in his rejection of the traditional cloistered judicial life-style seems to be too monocausational given all of the other influences in his life pushing him toward activism.[7] The most persistent theme running through the work, however, is the importance of his conquest of fear. It was his ability through self-discipline and the guidance of George Draper and others to develop ways to cope with fear that explains so much about Douglas's personal and judicial behavior. His poignantly relevant assertion that willfully manufactured political fears often lead to constitutional shortcuts reflects his continued awareness of the horribly destructive potential of fear.[8]

Although the work concentrates on describing the events in Douglas's life up to 1939, it actually extends much further because of his interesting, though sometimes distracting, habit that also appeared in *Of Men and Mountains* of interrupting the narrative to trace the impact of these earlier experiences on his more recent behavior. It is in these references that Douglas reveals an abiding sense of uneasiness about the emerging conservative, judicial-restraint-oriented majority of the Burger Court and the impediments to democracy he sees in the modern political process.[9] Though clearly in the realm of personal *obiter dicta*, these remarks are valuable for the contrast they present between Douglas's basic liberal values and those espoused by the spokesman for America's new conservative majority.

Go East, Young Man should prove to be of lasting value to persons with legal and political interests. The former will find Douglas's depiction of the evolution of his judicial realism particularly worthwhile. Though the specific experiences that pushed him in that direction were far different from those that affected Roscoe Pound, Louis Brandeis, Hugo Black, and others, he makes it clear that he shared with them the fundamental precept that law should be meaningfully related to the conditions of modern life.[10] This aspect of his thinking will be examined more carefully in the chapters on his legal thought and writings.

The value of Douglas's work for the political historian lies in the fresh perspective it provides on the complex mosaic of personalities involved in the New Deal. It is here that his anecdotal style is most effective. His contentions that Franklin D. Roosevelt would have been able to avoid our involvement in the Asian quagmire had he lived and that the witch hunt that later emerged in full bloom as McCarthyism was well under way prior to 1945 are provocative. His candid description of Felix Frankfurter's behavior prior to his appointment to the Supreme Court makes it clear that historians must avoid creating demigods out of mere men.[11] It underscores the lasting enmity between Douglas and Frankfurter, two strong-willed men with two sharply conflicting assumptions about the uses of judicial process as an agent of social change. In so doing, it also pinpoints the cause of a lot of the criticism aimed at Douglas's approach to the judicial process. *Go East, Young Man* illuminates the kind of controversies that were so common in Douglas's career and reminds the reader that they owe much to fundamental aspects of his personality.

Perhaps the most important aspect of Douglas's personal and literary perspective was shaped by his early experiences, described so poignantly in *Of Men and Mountains* and *Go East, Young Man.* The loss of his father at an early age, the poverty of his childhood, his attack of infantile paralysis, his conquest of its effects, his wilderness experiences, his academic excellence, and his struggle to pay for his education from high school through law school—all these and more shaped Douglas's attitude toward life. All pushed him toward self-reliance, created a competitive personality, and gave him a strong sense of self-confidence.[12]

It also created what was to become a central motif in his writing. His perception of the worth of challenge as a crucial element in his personal development and its accompanying corollary that individuals must confront and overcome their fears appear in all of the varied aspects of his writing. This is the direct result of his own experiences.[13] Though sometimes partially obscured by the nature of his subject matter, the application of this challenge motif to himself, other individuals, and widely varying groups is a constant in Douglas's writing. It provides structure and unity in the midst of his great topical variety.

One of his best discussions of the effect of challenge on his outlook on life appeared in a 1973 article in *Today's Health*. When asked to discuss the reasons for his vitality, he stated:

> In my own life challenge has played an important role. For years I had a deep-seated competitive drive that was motivated by crippling polio, which cost me the use of my legs from the time I was four until I was six. The desire to walk, to run, to walk thousands of miles was a burning force in my life. . . .
> Vitality, in many cases, is a response to challenges met and overcome.[14]

Emphasizing that the real keys to vitality were matters of the spirit and the mind as opposed to salable physical fitness, he resorted to one of his frequently used stylistic habits and listed the three greatest challenges to vitality in America. He ranked the commitment to violence, our saturation with material things, and the increasing regimentation of man as the major threats to the vitality of American life. The first was inspired by his more recent opposition to the war in Vietnam but the latter two were longstanding topics in his writing.[15] All posed difficult problems whose solutions would require much from Americans. He never forgot the lesson of his early years that life was full of challenges to be overcome.

Douglas also never forgot that he once had been poor and physically weak. His struggle to overcome the financial hardship that went with living on the wrong side of the tracks in Yakima, Washington, forced him to work hard. His efforts included "riding the rods" as he followed the fruit harvests in the Yakima Valley. This brought him into contact with migrant workers, railroad section hands, and others who made their living through hard physical labor. This, in turn, gave him a sense of identification with the struggles of ordinary Americans and a sense of compassion for the underdog.[16] Moreover, it exposed him to the radical IWW doctrines still circulating in the harvest fields, mining towns, and lumber camps of the West during his youth. This exposure left him unafraid of discussion of radical doctrines because he understood the frustration that led to their creation and that talk was not the same thing as action.[17]

Even more significantly, his youthful experiences left him with a healthy skepticism about the establishment. Though he helped create New Deal administrative government and rose to a place of power in it and the federal judicial establishment, he maintained his willingness to criticize government bureaucracy when it impinged on individual freedom.[18] Also related to his youthful experiences was the respect that he felt as a young man for the western maverick political tradition advocated by that group of western progressives and reformers known collectively as "The Sons of the Wild Jackass." Douglas was a great admirer of such members of that group as Senators William Borah of Idaho and Hiram Johnson of California. He was strongly attracted by the individualism and stubbornness associated with that tradition.[19]

These early attitudes had much to do, in turn, with the shaping of the approach to law that Douglas developed from 1922–1927 as a student at Columbia University, in two years as a practitioner in New York City and Yakima, and then as a young law professor at Columbia. They helped push him toward acceptance of the doctrine of legal realism.[20] That approach to law emphasized functionalism, its use as a problem solving device, and the requirement that law be relevant to contemporary situations and problems. He was too active and challenge-oriented to accept the tenets of the contrasting doctrine of legal formalism with its emphasis on *stare decisis* and timeless absolutes in human relations.

As Sidney Davis has noted, these tendencies were solidified because the Yale Law School, where Douglas taught from 1928–1934, was a hotbed of legal realism.[21] His colleagues there included Charles C. Clark, Robert Maynard Hutchins, and Thurman Arnold, who greatly reinforced the young professor's growing interest in the legal relationships between business and society, first stimulated when he studied and taught with Professors Underhill Moore and Carl Llewellyn at Columbia.[22] In that context, Douglas concentrated on the highly technical field of corporate receivership and bankruptcy reorganization. The intellectual atmosphere and the camaraderie at Yale were such, and the emphasis on legal realism was so overpowering, that Douglas found himself strongly attracted to the personalities and principles of its leading advocates.

Douglas's early experiences also drew him toward the ideas of Louis Brandeis. Two aspects of Brandeis's thought proved especially influential. Although, as Thomas Emerson has shown, Douglas was ultimately most impressed by Brandeis's belief in the importance of the First Amendment as the keystone of an open democratic society, the full impact of that influence was not to reveal itself until much later.[23] Initially, Douglas was most deeply impressed by Brandeis's economic beliefs as expounded in *Other People's Money and How the Bankers Use It,* where he emphasized the necessity of corporate responsibility to the public and his advocacy of sociological juris-prudence in his brief in *Muller* v. *Oregon.*[24]

To Douglas, such ideas seemed to actualize many of the doctrines of judicial realism. His attraction to the Brandeisian doctrines of corporate responsibility through regulation and the fear and distrust of corporate bigness became lasting parts of his economic beliefs.[25] The same was true for the functional approach to law that Brandeis personified. Douglas never abandoned either. They dominated his economic thinking and his attitude toward the judicial process, quite often combining in areas where those two subjects interacted. Both were consistent extensions of the deeply embedded senses of fair play and compassion for the underdog that he had developed in his youth. Brandeis was delighted when President Roosevelt chose Douglas to replace him on the Supreme Court upon his retirement in 1939. Douglas's subsequent writing proves that he remained true to Brandeisian principles. In so doing, Douglas has, as John Frank said, become a bridge from progressivism to modern liberalism.[26]

These, then, were the important ideals and working assumptions that Douglas developed in the early years of his life. They were already very much in evidence when as a rising young legal scholar he produced his initial published writings. They were still the distinguishing marks of his writing some forty-five years later.

II   *The Professor and the Pen*

William O. Douglas's earliest published writings included book reviews, law review articles, and a coauthored textbook. All were highly technical in nature, the products of the expertise he had developed in his research and teaching at Columbia and Yale University Law Schools in the complex fields of corporate bank-ruptcy, reorganization, and receivership. In terms of subject matter, Douglas's interests were light years removed from his later and greatest realm of contribution to American constitutional develop-ment. Nevertheless, some major aspects of his legal thought and his beliefs about the judicial process appear early in his career.

By the late 1920s, the young law professor had already created a considerable reputation for his research and for his highly successful course at the Yale Law School, where he used real cases and situations as the basis of a functional rather than a theoretical or formula-oriented approach to his subject matter. The textbook, *Cases and Materials on the Law of Corporate Reorganization*, that he coauthored with Carrol M. Shanks in 1931 reflects this realist position.[27] Douglas sought to make his students aware of the actual problems that they would confront in the real world.

His earliest book reviews also emphasized the usability and the practicality of the works being examined. Writing in the November 1927 issue of the *Illinois Law Review*, Douglas said:

It is one thing to start a machine and see it run. It is another thing to be able to operate a machine once started. It is one thing to learn how to allege in a petition an act of bankruptcy; . . . it is another to be able to recognize a fraudulent conveyance or preference.

He then proceeded to illustrate through a series of contrasts what the volume's highly theoretical approach lacked in practicality. He did admit, though, that the volume had some value for students because: "It quite accurately pictures to them the wheels going 'round, and seeing wheels go 'round may make a mechanic a more intelligent mechanic. But it stands to reason it does not make a mechanic."[28]

Again, writing in the March 1929 issue of the *Yale Law Journal* in the review of a book on damage cases, Douglas stated:

The preface states that the "editor has endeavored to show the law of damages as it is functioning in the present." He has been partly successful. It is doubted if it can ever be effectively done so long as one is chained to the "value" abstraction.[29]

Douglas advocated a new, more analytical, holistic approach to the questions surrounding the law of bankruptcy, one that placed them in their social and economic context.

Consider his words in a May 1929 review, where in criticizing a casebook he said:

Occasionally, however, reference is made to source material describing the environment out of which the cases come and setting forth the business problem with which the judicial process is dealing. A new case-book mode is being followed![30]

It was important to him that law students have casebooks based on actual rather than theoretical situations. He developed his thoughts about the need for this new approach to casebooks even further in a review in the February 1930 *Yale Law Journal*. In his discussion of a book on the law and practice of receivership, he asserted:

Most books of this scope have a tendency to be encyclopedic rather than analytical. The tendency is to treat the general principles, to note the common exceptions, and to make no serious attempt to subject the decisions to an analytical process in an endeavor to measure accurately the distance the decisions have moved from a given point or to judge with approximation the goal toward which they are likely headed.[31]

He left no doubt that his concept of law was use-oriented. Law, to Douglas, was even in its most technical aspects a dynamic entity that had to confront modern conditions with alternatives to the doctrine of *stare decisis*.

The same regard for the functional operation of the law in real situations appeared in the first full-length article Douglas published. His discussion of liability and risk published in 1929 provides an excellent example of this:

Above all it attempts to furnish an economic and social basis for a rule of vicarious liability and to substitute for apologiae, at best inarticulate, an analysis that at least attempts to relate the legal problem to its economic and social environment. Such dynamic treatment does not conclude that the decisions are wrong. It merely puts them on a basis that makes possible a clearer articulation and a more careful analysis of the issues.[32]

In his second article, he discussed ways to prevent the escape of liability through the device of setting up subsidiary corporations and letting them go bankrupt. In his summation he said:

As yet the subject is covered with a "mist of metaphors." Until the courts stop to analyze with more particularity the factors motivating their decisions before lapsing into phrases such as "alter ego" or "adjunct" or "instrumentality" there seems little hope of making prediction more certain than the foregoing.[33]

To Douglas, doctrinal consistency was dependent on increased understanding of the nature of the judicial process, including the motives of the judges involved.

Some indications of Douglas's own stylistic preferences also appear in his early reviews and articles. In a number of instances, he praised a work's style as a means of effective presentation. He stated his dislike of casebooks written as colorless digests. His early writing style was already characterized by clarity, brevity of expression, and disarming frankness despite the highly technical nature of its subject matter. The pertinent anecdote was already an important part of his approach to style.

The stock-market crash and ensuing Great Depression created a tremendous interest in questions dealing with corporate bankruptcy, receivership, and reorganization in both business and governmental circles. Douglas, already an acknowledged expert in these areas, published a series of articles and book reviews and coauthored a textbook in the early years of the Depression that added to his reputation. His growing stature in his field was recognized in 1932 when he was appointed to the Sterling Chair of Commercial and Corporate Law at Yale. His previous work in the Business Failures Project and his activities as Sterling Professor brought him to the attention of those in the national government who were seeking to develop regulatory measures correcting the malpractices in the business community that had contributed to the Great Depression.

Douglas's writings from 1930–1934 reveal the continued applica-tion of the principles of judicial realism and his growing conviction that means would have to be found to make the American business community more socially responsible. The textbook, *Cases and Materials on the Law of Corporate Reorganization,* was critically well received not only because of the high degree of interest in its topic but because of the practical approach it stressed. The book was a compilation of the materials Douglas and Shanks used in their Yale Law School course.[34] As one reviewer noted, the authors had emphasized that:

The whole subject of corporate reorganization is an involved interaction between legal precedents and business necessities. The sooner both lawyers and judges on the one hand and business men and bankers on the other recognize this dual character of corporate reorganization procedure, the sooner can we develop a clearly articulated and "fair" method of dealing with the large business failures.[35]

Douglas and Shanks thus presented in an entirely technical work the idea that the whole subject of corporate organization was not fixed, that there were dynamic elements at work and practical situations to be confronted.

The textbook proved the consistency between his earlier criticisms of others and the application of the principles of judicial realism in his own work. The case materials and the samples of equity and receivership documents included were all taken from actual cases. They were designed to illustrate the variety of demands put upon those who create and apply the law.

Douglas's active involvement in the previously cited Yale University Business Failures Project led to his coauthoring two long articles on the problems connected with the methodology used in it.[36] Emphasis was placed on the compilation of data on the causes of business failure that would be useful for those seeking to prevent such failures in the future. The two articles present a conscientious discussion of the strengths and failures of the multivariate analysis used in the project. They illustrate Douglas's interest in basing his conclusions on data as accurate as possible. More importantly, they reveal his interest in understanding ". . . current economic and social phenomena that have never been studied scientifically by analysing the factors involved, by tracing the social, economic and legal antecedents, and by estimating the causal processes."[37] In addition to his attraction to social science methodology, the articles reveal Douglas's interest in understanding the full socioeconomic context that gave rise to business problems.

Also evident in his earlier writing was an interest in comparative legal studies. In March 1931, he published a review of a book on the law of insolvency in British India. Douglas wrote: "That there is something to be gained from studying the experience of other nations in dealing with the same or similar phenomena of insolvency is now being more generally recognized." He wasted no time in illustrating its value. In his discussion of the book, he expressed agreement with the author's criticism of Indian bankruptcy agents who neglected to "investigate the conduct of the bankrupt."[38] That practice contrasted sharply with his own view that the bankrupt's behavior should be closely examined for the sake of his damaged creditors. Douglas's long-lasting interest in comparative legal studies had its origins in very practical motives.[39]

Evidence that he was becoming increasingly preoccupied with the question of social controls on business appeared in his review of Max Radin's *The Lawful Pursuit of Gain* in 1931. Douglas revealed the undecided state of his thinking on the question of legal controls in his discussion of that volume's central theme, the oral and legal aspects of the debtor-creditor relationship.

Yet from the viewpoint of those concerned with law in the technical sense the problems of morals are less acute than the problems of legal control. In fact the moral issue may not be in doubt. Yet the issue of legal control remains extremely debatable. Lawyers, courts, legislatures must face the latter.[40]

It is clear that the increasing pressure for business regulation during the Depression had its effect on him.

Nor was he willing to ignore the moral side of the question. In that same review, Douglas criticized the author for his lack of consideration of the types of moral restraints and standards imposed on economic activity by other elements in the society besides courts and governmental agencies. Speaking with an awareness that foreshadowed his subsequent activities on the New Deal's Securities and Exchange Commission, he said:

Yet in lawful or even unlawful pursuits of gain it is not to be doubted that a particular activity is held up to moral standards of groups other than governmental agencies. At times the sanction of the groups may have equal or greater force than the remote, latent sanction of a court.[41]

Douglas recognized the limits of judicial regulation. He hoped it would be offset by business willingness to discipline itself.

Douglas utilized data from the Business Failures Project and his own research on the types of procedures and reorganization growing out of bankruptcy as the basis of a whole spate of articles on that topic in 1932–1933.[42] In all of these, he argued the need to develop nondiscriminatory procedures to speed up the process and lessen the administrative burden of the bankruptcy process. All of the articles emphasized the need to consider the situation fairly in specific cases instead of relying on binding precedents that failed to reflect the realities created by the Depression.

In urging, for example, that wage-earning bankruptcy be left to the states, he said:

Not until bankruptcy is thought of as a congeries of problems, such as housing, home buying, small loans, collection methods, unemployment, medical costs, retail credit practices, instalment [sic] buying, automobile accidents, etc., rather than as an institution, will more effective control over these problems and their various agencies eventuate.[43]

That he was not radical and against creditors' rights was substantiated by his sympathetic discussion of their plight in his articles.

Writing in May 1933, he urged the use of equity powers to protect creditor claims in bankruptcy and reorganization cases.[44]

On October 11, 1932, Douglas addressed the Seventh Annual Conference of Referees in Bankruptcy. Speaking at a time when the United States was in the depths of the Depression and in the midst of the 1932 presidential campaign, Douglas was asked to comment on the wisdom of the flood of bankruptcy-relief legislation recently introduced in Congress. The resulting speech presents a clear picture of his economic and legal thinking in mid-Depression.[45] The speech was marked by Douglas's candor, witty use of anecdotes, and sense of certitude. It set the pattern for later Douglas speeches. It was also one of the first instances of what came to be a career full of speeches that were republished as articles. Ultimately, many of those articles became chapters in his books. It should not seem surprising to the reader, then, that many of Douglas's books were marked with conciseness and clearly enunciated arguments. For these reasons, Douglas's 1932 speech to the Referees in Bankruptcy will be discussed at length.

Douglas opened his speech with an anecdote about a defeated congressman who had been forced to take a job disguised as a baboon bumping into another disguised as a lion as a means of focusing the attention of his audience on the contrast between pre- and post-Depression thinking. He reminded his audience of the vast number of bankruptcy bills introduced or waiting introduction in the Congress. Referring to the current situation confronting the referees, he analogized: "Whether the mortality of these bills will be as great as the mortality of bills receivable in bankruptcy remains to be seen. I have a suspicion that it will not be" (p. 25). Such efforts, though, did not guarantee any basic changes in the attitudes and practices related to what he called ". . . this gigantic social and economic problem."

After assuring his audience that he was not the proponent of any bill, he stated his approach to the bankruptcy problem clearly: "In the interests of an enlightened legal order, however, I have deep concern; in the immobility of vested interests I have disrespect; and in the lethargy and timidity against experimentation, I have utter contempt" (p. 25). The Depression situation and his already broadened perception of the social and economic implications of bankruptcy combined to convince him of the need for changes in the approach to it. As he informed his audience, his participation in the Yale Business Failures Project had led him to think deeply about the role of bankruptcy in the American economic system. Douglas thus indicated his preoccupation with the more general social implications as opposed to the more narrow administrative aspects of the problem that the bankruptcy referees dealt with on a day-to-day basis.

His independence of mind and willingness to dissent from predominant views appeared in his discussion of what at that time was the Hastings bill, the leading bankruptcy reform proposal currently before the Congress. He sharply criticized those expert witnesses who had testified that the major problem in the bankruptcy field was to remove ambiguities, that it was merely a matter of making bankruptcy ". . . a less strenuous or less confusing game" (p. 26). He also rejected the American Bar Association's view that the present Bankruptcy Act should not be abandoned in favor of theoretical and untested innovations. That position violated one of his basic beliefs, that the laws should change to meet the needs of the times (p. 26). To Douglas, the important thing was that the system adequately articulate the social order. The past was not in itself a justification for preservation of a law in the light of socioeconomic change.

Douglas was also sharply critical of those who insisted that the Hastings bill violated sacred American principles. The proponents of the position, after all, failed to reveal just what sacred principles the proposed bill violated. He rejected the idea that the longevity of the thirty-four-year-old Bankruptcy Act made it an American principle, just as he did the idea ". . . that a trader, who makes his creditor take his chance of payment on the outcome of a game of craps, is entitled to a discharge as a matter of right" (p. 26). He was certain that such patriotic arguments buried basic questions that the Depression had raised about bankruptcy law under layers of emotion.

Turning to those who warned that government regulation meant the development of a huge federal bureaucracy, he argued that the problems attributed to it may or may not be real. Such an argument, he said, begged the question at issue. The real problem, he insisted, must be seen

. . . in terms of alternatives. What price beaurocracy [sic]? What price bankruptcy? . . . Is this beaurocracy [sic] merely an excuse to get jobs for the unemployed: or is it the method and only method of obtaining adequate social control over failures? (p. 26)

Douglas made it clear that he preferred to take the risk of bureaucratic red tape rather than forego innovation and experimentation. He would have no part of the hostility to change that marked the careers and attitudes of so many members of the legal profession.

Douglas addressed himself to what he felt was the central problem growing out of the bankruptcy situation. Knowledge of bankruptcy, what he called the background of ". . . the causes of their failures and the various considerations of public policy involved," was readily available now, whereas it had not been previously (p. 26). The problem, as he saw it, was that those testifying on the subject had not examined the extensive factual data available on the subject. This was tragic because "statistics will not supply answers to questions at issue. But they certainly go far to take much dispute out of the realm of guess work" (p. 27). His point was unmistakable: those who held a narrow conception of bankruptcy as an autonomous unit feared the statistical evidence that indicated it was part of an interrelated complexity of causal events and circumstances that might require new state or federal legislation to correct.

Douglas concluded with a call for informed action in the bankruptcy field: "The call I would make is one to realism. Let us study the scope of the problem and its component parts. . . . I would dislike to decide these bankruptcy questions in vacuo or on hunches" (p. 27). Though he admitted that knowledge of the problems associated with bankruptcy were too limited to legislate definitively, he did insist that there was enough information to "warrant legislating experimentally" (p. 27). Without that, Douglas warned, the institution of bankruptcy as part of the legal order would fall into disuse.

III *Advocate of Administrative Government*

The challenge of the Depression required more than passivity from a personality like that of Douglas. Still, as Leon Epstein has written in his study of Douglas's economic beliefs,

. . . Douglas was not suggesting that the structure of private capitalism, as such, should be drastically altered. Rather it is plain that Douglas merely wanted the capitalist system . . . to work in a manner that was, by his standards, fairer and more equitable.[46]

The triumph of judicial realism in Douglas's thinking had many important results.

One was that Douglas escaped the narrow, technical confines of his field of specialization. This broadened perspective was one based on the assumption that elements of social control through government regulation were both possible and necessary. The evidence that he had examined in the Yale Business Failures Project made him acutely aware of the larger relationship between business activities and other aspects of American society. In short, he already possessed some of the characteristic beliefs popular in Franklin D. Roosevelt's New Deal, a fact that had not escaped the attention of those who were formulating its economic policies in Washington.

Douglas's acknowledged expertise in the realm of business failures and reorganization as well as his sympathy for experimentation brought him to the attention of Joseph P. Kennedy, chairman of the newly formed Securities and Exchange Commission. That agency was one of the vast number of New Deal regulatory bodies designed to correct or prevent the conditions that led to the Depression. Its specific responsibility was regulation of the stock market and securities industry. In 1934 Douglas left Yale University at Kennedy's invitation to direct a study on investors' protective committee roles in business reorganization that became the basis of subsequent legislation.[47]

The initial contact where he revealed his sharp wit and sociability to those with whom he worked proved to be the propelling force behind his emergence as a prominent figure in the New Deal governmental structure. In 1936 he was appointed to the SEC and a year later he became its chairman, a position he held for two years. During that time he was a frequent guest at dinner parties and poker sessions attended by President Roosevelt and many of the leading members of his administration.[48] These contacts marked the beginning of a lasting friendship with Roosevelt and many of the other prominent New Dealers.

Douglas's work on bankruptcy and receivership, his role in the formulation of the Securities Exchange Act of 1934, and his subsequent actions as a SEC commissioner all illustrated the influence of Louis Brandeis's thinking on him. Though originally skeptical of Brandeis's specific approach to regulation, Douglas's experience in Washington and contact with Brandeis soon brought about a change of heart.[49] He became convinced that Brandeis's point about truth in securities was crucial and he strongly defended the Securities Exchange Act of 1933, which brought advertising in securities under SEC control.[50] His strong belief in legal realism made it easy for him to share Brandeis's beliefs in the uses of the law as an instrument of regulation, as a tool to control the dangers of bigness, and as a means to force public accountability of business for its actions. Writing in the *Yale Law Journal* in 1934, he discussed securities regulation in terms of its role as part of a more comprehensive total program of economic regulation, one that foreshadowed the policy he would pursue as a member of the SEC.[51]

Douglas's adherence to the Brandeisian approach became even more evident as he rose to prominence as one of the directors of the New Deal regulatory structure. His career on the SEC was a remarkable one marked by sharp confrontations with leaders of the securities industry over his active enforcement of SEC policies. He played an active role in shaping the Public Utility Holding Company Act of 1935, with its famous "death sentence" against the pyramiding of holding companies that had created so much financial havoc prior to 1929 in the utilities industry. His direct attack on the excesses of the stock market earned him the eternal enmity of significant elements of the American business community who favored self-regulation with no government supervision of the securities market.[52] Ironically, though he was regarded as an enemy by much of the business community, Douglas supported what he called self-regulation with a "police escort" by the SEC. In a later interview, Douglas's chief counsel when he was chairman of the SEC presented an excellent description of the dynamic nature of his leadership of that body and his willingness to stand up for his beliefs in the face of formidable arguments to the contrary.[53]

Douglas's years on the SEC proved that he could function effectively while surrounded by controversy. It is not an overstatement to say that he met tough problems head-on and seemed to enjoy them.

As Douglas rose to prominence in the New Deal administrative structure during the middle and later 1930s, his writing underwent a transition from the highly technical discussions of his earlier career to more general defenses of the goals and purposes of administrative government. It is possible to argue that this transition was a rationalization of his own changing career goals since his writings represent evolution of his thought in a direction not evident prior to the Depression and the coming of the New Deal. For whatever reason, it is also evident that Douglas's earlier concentration on the relationship of law to society expanded in the light of his increasing preoccupation with the more general aspects of policy choices confronting American democracy. Douglas, in short, had developed a sense of national perspective.

Democracy and Finance: Addresses and Public Statements of William O. Douglas, a compilation of Douglas's speeches and writings during his SEC career, was published in 1940 under the editorship of James Allen.[54] The work presents a clear picture of Douglas's economic philosophy through some twenty-five of his attempts to explain the role of the SEC to the public and the business community. Though the work is comprised mostly of speeches that generally make, as one reviewer noted, "dull reading," Douglas's careful thinking and the book's topical arrangement in part at least offset that fault.[55] This first volume of Douglas's writings was to be one of many of his publications that originated as speeches or lectures.

Democracy and Finance, as its title suggests, revolves around the relationship of finance to the needs of a democratic society. The work is divided into six parts. The first centers on Douglas's depiction of the problems in finance and his suggestions for reform. His calls for public accountability in all phases of business activity throughout his speeches clearly portray the influence of Louis Brandeis on his economic thought.[56] His analysis reflects a confident understanding of what went wrong in the business community that contributed to the Depression.

The second section deals with problems centering on the stock exchange and the role Douglas played in its 1937 reorganization. The third contains his discussion of public utilities and the strong case he made for their effective regulation. The fourth section on reform of corporate reorganization is a collection of Douglas's more technical recommendations for ways of instilling fairness in the post-Depression business world.[57] The fifth and sixth sections deal respectively with his advocacy of the virtues of administrative government and his beliefs about the necessity of getting American youth interested in pursuing the kind of legal education that would draw them to government service and strengthen the democratic ideal.

The result is a volume marked by Douglas's clear, concise style and seriousness of purpose, one filled with examples of his bluntness and candor. Missing, though, is the witty, anecdotal approach that would characterize so many of his later speeches and writings. The work, it should be remembered, was written by someone deeply embattled who used his speeches and articles as weapons in the frontlines of political combat.[58]

The work is significant for a number of specific reasons. It clearly portrays his attachment to the concept of administrative government expounded by the antimonopoly wing of the New Deal in the 1930s. It reflects Douglas's continuing close attachment not only to the old progressive antimonopoly tradition of Louis Brandeis but also to the later views of Thurman Arnold, who saw the corporation as the product of a complex set of relationships in the economic environment.[59]

The speeches and articles in it are indicative of his confidence in the place of enlightened, humane administrative government in the American democratic system. *Democracy and Finance* thus presents perspective on a critical aspect of New Deal thought by one of its most influential advocates and formulators. It underscores his hard-headed realism and dedication to the ideal of democracy early in his public career.

Douglas's enthusiastic support of administrative government in *Democracy and Finance* contrasts sharply with his later hostility to the practices of government bureaucracy.[60] This raises a critical question about the causes of that change. Part of the answer can be found in Douglas's response to changing times and another part in his conception of the nature of administrative government. The Depression years and the war that followed left America with a huge federal bureaucracy. The behavior and values of that bureaucracy seemed far removed from the kind of necessary controls that Douglas had developed and applied in his work on the SEC in the midst of grave economic emergency.

He saw administrative government as a process that could, if properly developed, be attuned to the needs of both the American people and the business community. More specifically, it was necessitated by the technical intricacies of the business-government relationship. Writing in October 1938, he described its major virtues:

. . . its ability to deal with technical, debatable, undefinable, or imponderable matters in a discretionary manner. It provides a realistic and sound alternative to hard and inflexible rules which proceed on the false assumption that right or wrong, black or white constitute the only choice.[61]

He pointed out that such an approach to government was subject to limits. Congressional control was assured because that body mandated the standards and authorized the discretionary powers of the regulatory agencies.

Douglas asserted confidently that administrative government was here to stay because it was America's way of dealing with contemporary social and economic problems. He warned of two challenges that the future would present. First, it demanded that business develop the publicly responsible, progressive leadership that would cause administrative powers to be used sparingly. Second, it required that Americans place the concept of public service high in its scale of values.[62] For the latter, Douglas envisioned a constant influx of youth to keep administrative government free from institutional decay and stagnation. What was needed was the growth of a tradition that sent our sons into government on a scale that rivaled those connected with business and the professions.

The administrative government that Douglas envisioned would be one that constantly reassessed the validity of the assumptions underlying its policies. Such an approach would prevent the bureaucracy from developing the habit of doing things in traditional ways, and it would keep government administrators thinking in terms of the dynamic changes going on around them.[63] Douglas was obviously not blind to the challenges involved in preserving the vitality of administrative government, even in the period when he was most enthusiastic about its potential. The subsequent failure of administrative agencies to develop in the ways that he hoped disappointed him deeply.

This, when compounded by his growing interest in defense of individual freedoms, his reaction against the high-handed actions and the conservative policies of bureaucrats during the Cold War era, and the destructive effects of their policies on wilderness conservation proved too much for him to bear. Especially galling to Douglas were the probusiness appointments to the regulatory commissions.[64] Whether Douglas abandoned administrative government or it abandoned him is perhaps a moot question. The result was the same. *Democracy and Finance* presented a graphic picture of his early high hopes for that technique. It is a significant work because it provides a basis of comparison to gauge his optimism and idealism about the future of the New Deal and the depths of his later disappointments. It stands as a ringing defense of the role he played in shaping the administrative state.

By 1939, however, Douglas had decided because of the financial demands of his growing family to give up the SEC chairmanship and return to the more lucrative and less hurried life of a law professor at Yale. His desire to return to academia was permanently thwarted when President Roosevelt, seeking to fill his Supreme Court appointments with loyal New Deal liberals, accepted the advice of Senator William E. Borah of Idaho and appointed Douglas to the Supreme Court in 1939.[65] The seat Douglas received was that left vacant by the resignation of his hero and mentor, Louis Brandeis.

There is no doubt that Douglas's appointment to the Court was the critical turning point in his career. It guaranteed his place in public service and gave him a position of highest status in the American legal profession. As his experiences and writings proved during his record long stay on the court, it did not mean that he removed himself from the arena of public discussion and controversy. Justice Douglas's service on the Court, though critical, was only one aspect of his numerous interests, many of which in subsequent years would determine the important topics and shape the thesis of his voluminous writings in the postwar years.

CHAPTER 2

The Justice and the War

DOUGLAS'S early years on the Court saw America's increasing involvement and eventual participation in World War II. The impact of these events on Douglas's thinking is clearly evident in his opinions on the bench and his other writings during the war years. His patriotic enthusiasm undoubtedly inhibited his emergence as a civil libertarian on the Court and totally dominated the subject matter of his extralegal writings.

I   His Off-the-Bench Writings

Douglas's extralegal writings during the war clearly illustrated his growing conviction that America's primary goal should be the destruction of German and Japanese fascism and militarism. Virtually all of his off-the-bench writings were originally speeches designed to gain support for the war effort. He felt so strongly about the war that he considered resigning from the Court, as did his fellow Justice Frank Murphy, in order to take a position more directly involved in the war effort.[1] The Second World War presented Douglas with a challenge of massive proportions. It was one that he could not ignore.

A large number of Douglas's wartime speeches and statements were published in 1948 in *Being an American*.[2] The volume was compiled by Richard J. Walsh as a sequel to the earlier *Democracy and Finance*. It includes selections on the war effort, civil liberties, foreign policy, and the legal profession. As one reviewer noted, the book might have been intended as a campaign biography for what proved to be the abortive attempt of some liberals to make Douglas the Democratic party's presidential candidate in 1948.[3] Regardless of its intended use, the selections in *Being an American* illuminate many aspects of Douglas's thinking in the 1939–1949 period. Of immediate importance, however, is the significance of the book for the insights it presents about Douglas's wartime writing.

Douglas's wartime literary efforts were a form of propaganda. All were designed to create support for the American war effort. Most were homilies of cherished American values that required protection from the challenge of totalitarianism. Viewed collectively, they possess a thematic unity: the need to actively defend the democratic ideals that distinguished America and her allies from their enemies.

The bulk of Douglas's wartime speeches were presented in the first section of the book, appropriately subtitled "The American Idea." A number of representative examples will illustrate the richness of his expository techniques. In an address to graduates at William and Mary College on June 6, 1940, entitled "The Jeffersonian Philosophy," Douglas emphasized the importance of protecting democracy for minority dissenters as well as those who held the majority view because so many great ideas had emerged from dissenting thought. Emphasizing the importance of individual conscience on the American way of life, Douglas presented one of his favorite personal beliefs: man is only strong when free (pp. 18, 35).[4]

In the midst of his call for toleration of dissent, he drew an analogy between Jefferson and the Founding Fathers being forced to fight for their freedom just as modern Americans were being forced to do. Americans, he said, ". . . cannot neglect their duty and allow aggressors to overrun the earth" (p. 18). Douglas closed his William and Mary address with a reminder that the native American traditions of respect for individuals, common sense, ample economic opportunity, individual initiative, and fair play represented ample materials to create the democracy of the future without importing other types of thought. The merger of his own beliefs with what he perceived as American ideals seemed complete in his wartime speeches.

In another speech, "The Tradition of Equality," given at the dedication of a hydroelectric dam on the Columbia River in 1942, Douglas again made use of a historical analogy. He likened the pioneer experience of the past to the modern American fight against despotism and tyranny for a "new right to freedom" (p. 21). The war effort, with its common purpose of struggle, he predicted, would reinforce feelings about the brotherhood of man. From the crucible of war would emerge a better nation. Turning to more immediate things, Douglas praised the vast resources of his beloved Pacific Northwest and called the dam he was dedicating an ". . .

instrumentality of war for the preservation of freedom" (p. 23). The combination of support for the war effort and advocacy of democratic ideals permeated his speeches.

Douglas's view of American responsibilities to the rest of the world during the war was not a narrow one. In a speech entitled "Freedom" given on May 28, 1942, at Washington and Jefferson College, he reminded Americans that it was their responsibility to carry the concept of freedom to the peoples of the world. Here, for the first time, he enunciated with near-evangelical fervor the need to spread the message of freedom, a theme that appeared again and again in his later writings on America's role in world affairs (p. 26).[5]

He emphasized that there had been many bloody interludes in the American struggle for freedom. Even though the enemy was "thorough and calculating" he had failed to ". . . perceive the deep sources of our spiritual strength" in what had turned into a "total war" (p. 27). The successful end of the war, he warned, would not mean the end of the struggle for freedom. It would, he insisted, call for a cooperative effort rather than an imperialistic approach, one that would ". . . eradicate the disease of aggression by going to the root of the infection." Douglas made use of President Roosevelt's expression to remind his audience that they had a "rendezvous with destiny" to underscore the importance of America's role in world affairs (p. 28). His growing concern for a system of international cooperation proved to be one of the main tenets of his postwar approach to American foreign policy.

Another of Douglas's more significant wartime speeches, "A Nation of Minorities," was given on March 1, 1943, to the American Jewish Congress. It was a rebuttal of German and Japanese propaganda that emphasized the discrimination against minorities in the United States. He argued that it was critically important that the rights of the smallest minority in America, the individual conscience, be defended and the Bill of Rights that guaranteed it be preserved. History has shown, he noted, that Adolf Hitler would not understand a society when an individual could stand alone. He warned that the persecution of any minority would create a rationale for the persecution of others and that the practice would spread like a blight. For that reason, there must be no persecution of any minority. He concluded idealistically that Americans were a nation of minorities who had to live, work, and stick together.

The question of minority rights was far more than a theoretical one for Douglas and his brethren on the Court. His writings off the bench contrasted with his ambiguous behavior regarding the internment of Japanese-Americans. His agonized attempt to come to grips with that problem is discussed in a later part of this chapter.[6] His writing illustrates the collision of conflicting values and loyalties involved in his reaction to the Japanese issue.

The speeches that comprise *Being an American* go beyond the realm of mere propaganda. The traditional calls for courage and sacrifice are reinforced with a plea for something more: the courage to live the ideals that Americans advocated (pp. 107–12). Totalitarianism, to Douglas, represented a deadly threat to basic American freedom. That was the essence of the challenge Douglas saw in the Second World War.

The speeches also reveal Douglas's awareness of questions of civil rights during the war years, even though his judicial record in that period is not consistent. As one reviewer noted about the speeches in *Being an American*: "Mr. Douglas reveals himself as a phrasemaker with eloquent and optimistic devotion to Civil Rights and the well-being of the common man. These excerpts also hint at considerable understanding of the requirements for true political democracy."[7] His faith in American ideals helped to create in his writing a clear perception of the enemy and a strong rationale for supporting the war effort. To Douglas, the Second World War, not the First, was the war that would make America, if not the rest of the world, safe for democracy.

The product of a particular time period with its own unique emotions, the speeches seem dated to today's readers and perhaps, in the wake of our disillusionment about our involvement in Vietnam, very naive. This is especially true when we realize that Douglas moved away from support of subsequent American military efforts and that he became an unrelenting critic of our involvement in Vietnam, even supporting efforts to get the question of the constitutionality of our involvement before the Supreme Court.[8]

What happened later, however, should not prevent us from understanding the ability of Douglas and millions of other Americans during World War II to become enthusiastic supporters of the war effort. Douglas's wartime speeches thus remind us of the experiential gulf that separates "then" from "now." They also reveal the value of the study of transitions in Douglas's writings to bridge the gap from the present to the not too distant past. The

impact of changing times even on writers like Douglas, who are
known for the consistency of their theme and style, must not be
overlooked.

II   Douglas on the Wartime Court:
The War Effort and Regulation

Two major themes run through Douglas's wartime Supreme
Court opinions, his initial ones on the Court. These decisions prove
his devotion to the war effort and New Deal regulatory policies.
Inadvertently, his preoccupation with these subjects greatly inhibited the judicial application of the previously cited civil libertarianism that he advocated so passionately in his speeches on behalf of
the war effort.[9] The result was a somewhat mixed record on civil-
liberties issues in his written opinions.

Though Douglas came to the Supreme Court after the great
Court-packing fight in 1937, when it had accepted the doctrines of
liberal nationalism, his first years on the bench were still in the
period when the regulatory structure of the New Deal was being
legitimatized through a number of case precedents. As C. Herman
Pritchett noted, the "Roosevelt Court" was composed of diverse
personalities who had sharp disagreements about the nature and
uses of the judicial process. Nevertheless, nearly all of them accepted
with varying degrees of enthusiasm the government regulatory
policies in the war years.[10] Because of Douglas's expertise in the
area of business regulation, it became his lot to author the complex
opinions on many of the diverse aspects of the business-government
relationship. Though he was a fast worker, such cases because of
their complexity and number absorbed much of his attention and
time.[11]

Douglas's strong proregulatory stance in both his majority opinions and occasional dissents was the result of his Brandeisian
economic beliefs and his more recently acquired sense of obligation
to restrict interference with the government's war power.[12] References to a number of his more representative cases will illustrate
this aspect of his on-the-bench writings. Such an approach obviously
cannot replace reading Douglas's opinions in the *United States
Supreme Court Reports,* where the points of fact and law in the
cases as well as the interaction of conflicting and concurring justices'
arguments make both cases and opinions more understandable.
Only in that way can the reader experience the complexity, chal-

lenge, and significance of American constitutional interpretation and Douglas's role in shaping it.

In typical New Deal style, Douglas wrote or joined opinions upholding the extension of congressional regulatory authority. These included granting Congress the power to regulate pricing and competitive methods in the coal industry and upholding government construction and control of dams for flood control and electric power. He also joined in opinions upholding federal farm policies and the validity of wage and hours legislation.[13] In all of these cases, Douglas relied on a broad view of the scope of the interstate commerce power to support his opinion.

And so it went in the vast majority of his opinions involving government regulation of business. His antitrust opinions, for example, present a similar pattern, revealing a very expansive view of the scope of government regulatory power. Writing in *United States* v. *Socony-Vacuum Oil Co.* in 1940, Douglas revealed his expansive interpretation of the Sherman Antitrust Act and also a great deal about his beliefs in the need for business competition.[14] Douglas ruled in the opinion that price-fixing agreements were illegal per se and that such agreements did not have to be proven to be in restraint of trade as many argued. He explained his position in the following manner:

If the so-called competitive abuses were to be appraised here, the reasonableness of prices would necessarily become an issue in every price-fixing case. In that event the Sherman Act would soon be emasculated; its philosophy would be supplanted by one which is wholly alien to a system of free competition; it would not be the charter of freedom which its framers intended.[15]

Enforcement of broadly interpreted antitrust legislation, Douglas believed, would protect the public from the curse of bigness by encouraging open competition. As in his work on the SEC, Douglas applied government regulation as something that protected rather than harmed capitalism.

Douglas also joined the Court majority in the controversial *South-Eastern Underwriters Assn.* case when it held that the life insurance business was part of interstate commerce and subject to federal regulation even though it had been traditionally considered a state matter.[16] His opinions in antitrust cases in the postwar years revealed the extension of the trend. In one such case, *United States*

v. *Columbia Steel Co.* in 1948, Douglas attacked vertical integration in the steel industry.[17] Dissenting against the Court's ruling that such integration did not violate the Sherman Antitrust Act, Douglas said:

We have here the problem of bigness. Its lesson should by now have been burned into our memory by Brandeis. The Curse of Bigness shows how size can become a menace—both industrial and social. It can be an industrial menace because it creates gross inequalities against existing or putative competitors. It can be a social menace—because of its control of prices. Control of prices in the steel industry is powerful leverage on our economy.[18]

His perception of the broad scope of the Sherman Act was consistent: its major aim was the control of bigness.

Quite expectedly, the same pattern of support for regulation appeared in his numerous opinions in cases involving the war power. He joined the majority in upholding price controls in one decision and wrote a majority opinion upholding their application in another. Writing in the latter case, he said:

To require hearings for thousands of landlords before any rent control order could be made effective might have defeated the program of price control. Or Congress might well have thought so. National security might not be able to afford the luxuries of litigation and the long delays which preliminary hearings traditionally have entailed.[19]

He felt so strongly about the need for sweeping application of such controls that he dissented sharply against the trend of the Court's majority late in the war to ease their application in certain instances. He presented his rationale for such a rigid view in *Davies Warehouse Co.* v. *Bowles* in 1944.

Every exception read into the Act creates another point of leakage, multiplies the task of enforcement, and creates a favored class of businesses. I would not read the Act with such a hostile eye. Where two interpretations are possible I would take the one which avoids those results. The choice between the "letter" and the "spirit" is an ancient one even in the law.[20]

In this case and other dissents, Douglas expressed his intense opposition to any policy that would give a business an opportunity to exploit wartime conditions.[21] Such policies all worked to inhibit the government's war effort.

The degree of Douglas's devotion was further illustrated in a number of cases where he held in favor of national regulatory power when it conflicted with similar state power. Writing in *Penn Dairies* v. *Milk Control Commission of Pennsylvania* in 1942, he explained his views in a dissent:

> We have then regulations of the War Department made pursuant to powers delegated by Congress and which prohibit the Army's contracting officers from waiving competitive bidding merely because prices are fixed by the states. I am unable to see why they are not valid regulations. . . .
> These War Department regulations accordingly "have the force of law." Their application in this case therefore has no less force and effect than if it was specifically directed by Congress. We have then an assertion of federal power in the field of price control which by reason of the supremacy clause excludes any exercise of a conflicting state power.[22]

It is important to remember that one of Brandeis's favorite hopes was that the states should be permitted great leeway in pioneering social and economic measures in as many instances as possible.[23] Also, Douglas's view here sharply contradicted his own earlier position that many matters such as individual bankruptcy and some form of business regulation should be left to the states. This aspect in particular illustrates the preeminence that support of the war effort occupied in his scale of wartime priorities.

Despite the above exception, there was one aspect of Douglas's wartime opinion writing that proved beyond a doubt his continued adherence to Brandeisian economic doctrine and his intention that it be implemented. Douglas used his case opinions on utility-rate regulation to write into constitutional law ideas developed by Brandeis some twenty years previously. Since the early 1900s, the Court had held in a series of cases that it was unconstitutional for a regulatory commission or a state legislature to set utility prices that were "unreasonable."[24]

When the Court developed the "rule of reason," they evolved a whole series of corollaries to it. As John Frank has noted:

> The most astounding of these was that the rate fixed must take into account and allow a return on the wholly fictitious reproduction cost of the utility. With prices generally on a rising curve in the United States, this meant that utilities were guaranteed a return based on an assumption that a utility might be reconstructed at higher prices than we ever expended in building it in the first place.[25]

The probusiness Supreme Court majority of the 1920s had assailed Brandeis and Holmes's argument that rates should be based on the amount "prudently invested" in the utility and that their return should be pegged at the differing sums necessary for each utility to operate efficiently.

Douglas, early on in his career, became convinced that the Brandeis-Holmes approach was much more beneficial to the public interest than was the "rule of reason." Consequently, he concurred in one case decision and wrote the majority opinion in another, *Federal Power Commission* v. *Hope Natural Gas Co.* in 1944, that swung the Court over to the Brandeis-Holmes approach to rate-fixing.[26] In the *Hope* case, Douglas upheld the Federal Power Commission's fixing of the rate of return at 6 percent of the depreciated actual investment of the company, a figure roughly half of the amount claimed by it under the old method of computing rates.

Douglas announced the majority's acceptance of the new approach in clear, concise language, junking the "rule of reason" guidepost as formerly applied.

Under the statutory standard of "just and reasonable" it is the result reached not the method employed which is controlling. It is not theory but the impact of the rate order which counts. If the total effect of the rate order cannot be said to be unjust and unreasonable, judicial inquiry under the Act is at an end.[27]

The public utilities were thus shorn of the protective cover provided by the "rule of reason." Douglas had struck what he felt was a fairer balance between investor and consumer interest. Such decisions and his previous actions on the SEC made bitter and lasting enemies for him in the American business community and among its journalistic allies.[28]

There was one area of notable exceptions to Douglas's profederal regulatory posture. Though he supported the Interstate Commerce Commission in cases that contested the scope of its powers, Douglas exhibited a marked hostility to the administrative actions of that body. He and a number of other liberals felt that the ICC was dominated by big-business and railroad interests who used their powers against the smaller operators and the trucking industry in order to encourage monopoly and concentration rather than to seek their prevention.[29] Despite these feelings, or perhaps because of them, he chose to center his opinions on the procedural and administrative flaws in the ICC's actions.

Writing in *Gregg Cartage Co.* v. *United States*, Douglas showed his dissatisfaction with the commission's action excluding truckers from the so-called "Grandfather Clause" in the Motor Carrier Act of 1935.[30] Exclusion from that clause prevented a trucker from carrying goods back to the South after he had delivered products to northern states. A trucker would, in effect, be driving empty half of the time.

In overturning the decision, Douglas, speaking for the majority, said:

Great deference is owed a commission's interpretation of the law which it enforces, especially where the meaning of the statutory language, generally or in specific application, gains body and flavor from the content of the highly specialized field in which the expert body works. . . . But that is quite different from acceding to the suggestion that the non-technical word "control" may be interpreted in a way which goes against all human experience and which does violence to its ordinary and accepted meaning. . . . We should not permit . . . statutory grants to be whittled away on the basis of technical and legalistic grounds which find no expression in the statute however much the administrative chore may be alleviated.[31]

The crucial point for Douglas was the effect of the ICC's action on the independent trucker involved in the case.

As Douglas said in another case, the practical result of such commission action was critical because: "To appellee such matters involves life or death. Empty or partially loaded trucks on return trips may well drive the enterprise to the wall." For this reason, Douglas held that

. . . the precise grounds for the Commission's determination . . . are not clear. . . . The defect is not merely one of the absence of a "suitably complete statement" of the reasons for the decisions; it is the "lack of the basic or essential findings required to support the Commission's order."[32]

The vague wording of the grant of power to the ICC enabled Douglas to attack its behavior on technical grounds.

In another opinion, Douglas called for more comprehensive attention to the needs of competition when judging the effects of business consolidation. Writing in dissent from the Court when it upheld the ICC's approval of a merger on the grounds that it had acted properly since such consolidation was exempt from antitrust legislation under the Transportation Act of 1935, Douglas made it clear that he was deeply opposed to bigness:

> . . . I would resolve the ambiguities of the Act in favor of the maintenance of free enterprise. If that is too niggardly an interpretation of the Act, Congress can rectify it. But if the Commission is allowed to take the other view, a pattern of consolidation will have been approved which will allow the cartel rather than the competitive system to dominate this field. History shows that it is next to impossible to turn back the clock once such a trend gets under way.[33]

The justice was not afraid to substitute his own impression of what was good for the public interest for that of the commission. There are no clearer expressions of his Brandeisian approach than those presented in his usually critical opinions in cases where the ICC showed sympathy for consolidation.

It is safe to argue, as Professor Leon Epstein has in his seminal article on Justice Douglas's economic beliefs, that his writings reflect the result-oriented jurisprudence that was one of the important traits of judicial realism. As Epstein states:

> Justice Douglas is a staunch supporter of a New Deal type of government regulation of business, that he favors such regulation whether it is in the hands of national or state authorities, and that in the case of conflict between the two authorities he is likely to prefer that which champions the stronger regulatory policy.[34]

Douglas's case opinions were heavily reinforced by his own experiences in the New Deal. Moreover, his enthusiastic support of the war effort and his resultant broad definition of the federal government's war powers added strength to his rationale for the use of such powers in the business community.

There are, as with all justices, signs of inconsistency in his more than 1,200 judicial opinions. In Douglas's case, however, the economic and regulatory beliefs that appeared in his opinions in the war years remained the basis of his approach to economic issues for the rest of his career.[35]

Douglas's style in his early legal opinions reflects the successful transference of the concise, lucid approach developed in his earlier writings to the realm of case opinions. The available evidence suggests that he worked hard on his style, treasuring opinions that stated their points "very clearly and succinctly."[36] As both his critics and defenders have noted, Douglas's opinions were not filled with legal or technical jargon or stilted phraseology. He stated the facts and points of law involved in the case before him and attempted to dispose of it forthwith. A great number of Douglas's decisions were, as John Frank pointed out, ". . . concise, totally knowledgeable both of the facts and the law, and completely comprehensible."[37] His writing style here manifests traits in his personality, as can best be appreciated by reading extensively in Douglas's case opinions.

III   *Douglas on the Wartime Court: The Civil Liberties Opinions*

The consistency that characterized Douglas's economic decisions was decidedly lacking in his civil-liberties opinions during the war years. The war created a grave crisis in the justice's legal thought. It resulted in an inevitable clash between government power and individual freedom. Consequently, Douglas, in many civil-liberties cases during the war, succumbed to the demands of national security in spite of the frequent calls in his wartime speeches for the vigorous application of the Bill of Rights.[38]

A survey of Justice Douglas's approach to civil liberties in the war years is complicated by another problem. Unlike his persistent habit in later years of writing separate opinions explaining his views, Douglas did not ordinarily follow that practice during the war. As L. A. Powe, Jr., has observed: ". . . he ordinarily joined in the Court's majority opinion; and in those rare instances when Douglas himself authored opinions in the first amendment area, they were written—with only one exception—for the Court."[39] What this means is that there is room for much educated guesswork about Douglas's thinking on civil-liberties matters in the war years. One thing is certain, however. There was little if anything in Douglas's opinions in that period that suggested his eventual acceptance of the absolutist view of First Amendment rights that marked his case opinions and judicial writings in more recent years.

His few written opinions in cases dealing with both state and federal restrictions of First Amendment freedoms were dominated by the concept of balancing individual versus government rights. The chasm standing between that approach to constitutional inter- pretation and one based on absolutism was so vast that it would require time and considerable doctrinal experimentation to bridge it. Douglas's case opinions and legal writings provide a fascinating picture of his journey from balancing to absolutism as the basis of his approach to First Amendment freedoms.[40]

That journey has to be understood against the backdrop of the growing interest of the United States Supreme Court in civil liberties and the constitutional doctrines developed in response to it. World War II caught the Court in the midst of the long process of incorporating the different amendments in the federal Bill of Rights into restrictions upon the states through the due-process clause of the Fourteenth Amendment. The Court's behavior in the war years revealed that there was a great deal of judicial latitude concerning what constituted the scope of the freedoms contained in the phrases of the First Amendment. Shortly before Douglas's appointment to the Court, questions about freedom of expression and the free exercise of religion had started coming to the Court. These were stimulated by the activities of labor organizations on one hand and the Jehovah's Witnesses on the other.[41] In a series of initial cases, including *Lovell* v. *Griffin* and *Hague* v. *CIO*, the Court had struck down state and local attempts to forbid the distribution of handbills for religious purposes and the prevention of public meetings for labor union organizing.[42]

By the time Douglas came to the Court, more complex cases were coming to it, ones in which the question of "relevant state interests" were also being forcefully argued. Douglas went along with the Court's rejection of that argument in *Thornhill* v. *Alabama* in 1940 when it struck down a state law forbidding all picketing as a violation of freedom of expression protected by the First Amendment.[43] Yet, when Douglas authored his initial First Amendment opinion in *Teamsters Local 802* v. *Wohl* in 1942, he admitted that picketing was something more than speech and that it could be regulated to insure its peaceful application:

Picketing by an organized group is more than free speech, since it involves patrol of a particular locality and since the very presence of a picket line may induce action of one kind or another, quite irrespective of the nature of the ideas which are being disseminated. Hence those aspects of picketing make it the subject of restrictive legislation.[44]

To Douglas, sweeping legislation on picketing could conceivably be a form of prior restraint but the unique nature of picketing made it necessarily subject to some control for the good of society.

Similarly, his approach to the troubling questions surrounding the activities of Jehovah's Witnesses was marked by variation and a balancing of interest. He had no difficulty in concurring with the Court when it invalidated a law requiring permits to pass out handbills in *Schneider* v. *State* and a law that allowed an official to determine whether a religious group was bona fide in *Cantwell* v. *Connecticut.*[45] Two weeks after the *Cantwell* decision, however, Douglas voted with the Court to uphold the state's position in *Minersville School District* v. *Gobitis*, the first of the so-called Flag Salute cases involving the refusal of the Jehovah's Witnesses to pledge allegiance. In the decision, Douglas voted with the majority when it held to Justice Felix Frankfurter's dictum that ". . . national unity is the basis of national security."[46] Again in 1941, Douglas went along with the decision in *Cox* v. *New Hampshire* that upheld the conviction of sixty-eight Jehovah's Witnesses for participating in a parade without a permit.[47] The Court cited the absence of arbitrary administrative power and the importance of maintaining public order by controlling street traffic as the basis of its decision.

When the issue of regulation of the Jehovah's Witnesses' sale of their literature came to the Court, that body, after some hesitation, held in 1943 that distribution of religious handbills advertising the sale of certain books was within the realm of freedom of expression protected by the First Amendment. The next First Amendment opinion that Douglas wrote, *Murdock* v. *Pennsylvania*, did this ". . . by applying a functional test to commercial speech, with the key emphasis on the vendor's purpose."[48] Yet, in applying the test in *Murdock*, he held that

. . . an age-old form of missionary evangelism . . . occupies the same high estate under the First Amendment as do worship in churches and preaching from the pulpits. . . . The mere fact that the religious literature is "sold" by itinerant preachers rather than "donated" does not transform evangelism into a commercial enterprise.[49]

Douglas's decision in *Murdock* thus seems to shift back and forth between the area of free expression of speech and free exercise of religion.[50]

That he had resolved his indecision on what part of the Constitution to base his pamphlet-peddling opinions became clear in the following year in *Follett* v. *Town of McCormick*.[51] In that decision, Douglas extended the freedom to sell pamphlets to include both itinerant and resident evangelists, resting his decision on the free exercise of religion principle. It is plausible to argue, as Powe does, that Douglas's sympathy to the Witnesses in the cases just cited, those dealing with municipal taxing ordinances, also explains his changed stance in *West Virginia State Board of Education* v. *Barnette*, the second Flag Salute case. He feared that the ordinances in all three of the cases, though neutral on their face, could be used as weapons to single out one unpopular minority "for disguised religious persecution."[52]

Lest this be taken as an argument against the general hypothesis that Douglas's opinions reflect a balancing process between individual rights and state powers, it should be remembered that Douglas joined the majority in *Prince* v. *Massachusetts* in 1944.[53] That opinion upheld the conviction of a Witness for violating the Massachusetts Child Labor Statute by permitting her nine-year-old ward to sell religious literature. Whether Douglas felt there was less chance of persecution under that law or that it was necessary to preserve the state's ability to prevent exploitation of children or that he thought both were germane, the result was the same. His vote was the result of the balancing process he applied in the war years to the civil-liberties cases involving state action.

The same pattern of response that marked Douglas's behavior in these cases also characterized those involving federal powers and civil rights. The justice maintained his habit of joining other justices' opinions and actually authored only one First Amendment–federal-power decision during the war. His votes in the First Amendment cases indicate that he continued to utilize the balancing process in deciding between the demands of personal freedom and government powers, though he was more reluctant to vote against the federal government than the states.[54]

Douglas joined the Court's majority in voting to uphold the licensing authority of the Federal Communications Commission despite the argument of the National Broadcasting Company that such regulations impinged on freedom of speech.[55] He also joined the dissent in two cases that raised freedom-of-speech issues relating to the war effort when the Court limited the government's power. His first vote came in *Viereck* v. *United States* when the Court interpreted the Foreign Agents Registration Act as not requiring a registered agent to disclose his own propaganda activities as opposed to those of his foreign clients.[56] In this case Douglas agreed with Justice Hugo Black's argument that the agent should still register with the government so as to make the American people aware that he was not necessarily acting as a disinterested person.

His second dissent came in *Hartzel* v. *United States* when an appeal from an espionage conviction reached the Court.[57] The majority found insufficient evidence to convict Hartzel, who had written a series of pamphlets prior to and after American entry into the war filled with racist overtones and calls for a German victory that he had sent to military commanders and persons registered for the draft. Douglas supported Justice Stanley F. Reed's dissenting argument that Hartzel's behavior was an attempt to obstruct the armed forces and was, therefore, punishable under the Espionage Act. Thus, the evidence suggests, as in the state cases, that he applied a balancing process and refused to allow actions that would threaten the government's ability to carry on the war effort.

Douglas's lone written wartime opinion in the First Amendment–federal-power area came in *United States* v. *Ballard*.[58] The defendant in the case, the leader of the "I Am" religious movement, had been convicted of mail fraud for selling books, records, and paintings with the claim that they had supernatural qualities. Douglas, in overturning the defendant's conviction, ruled that the jury had no right to determine the truth or falsity of his religious beliefs but only whether he believed them.[59] Here again, rather than writing off the whole question of an examination of personal beliefs as something prohibited by the First Amendment, as Justice Robert Jackson urged, Douglas and the Court's majority did not deny the right of the government to prosecute. Instead, they developed a criterion for balancing off such interests with the sincerity of those involved, a matter of great difficulty to determine.

Nowhere was the tension created by that process more evident than in Douglas's concurring opinion when the Court, relying on extremely narrow procedural grounds, upheld the legality of the United States government's curfew order for the West Coast Japanese in *Hirabayashi* v. *United States* in 1943.[60] He also voted with the Court's majority to uphold the order excluding the Japanese from the Coast in *Korematsu* v. *United States* in 1944.[61] Douglas, who had grown up in the Pacific Northwest, had great personal sympathy with the Japanese and was acutely aware of the prejudice directed against them by white Americans living along the West Coast.[62] He made his disagreement with such behavior clear in a letter to Chief Justice Harlan F. Stone in which he said: "Racial solidarity and lack of assimilation do not show lack of loyalty as I see it."[63] His concern about this point was not the controlling factor at that time, however.

He was also willing to grant that the American military was acting in good faith when it decided that the speed of its actions was more important for national security than immediately distinguishing the loyal from the disloyal Japanese. As he said in his *Korematsu* concurrence: "We cannot say that the war making branches of the Government did not have ground for believing that in a critical hour such persons could not readily be isolated and separately dealt with. . . ."[64] The primacy of the war effort was evident in Douglas's actions.

Signs of his uneasiness about the resulting internment of the Japanese could be seen in his encouragement of individual Japanese to file habeas corpus suits in federal district courts to gain release from the camps.[65] Douglas's 1944 majority opinion in *Ex parte Endo* upheld that approach.[66] His opinion carefully avoided ruling on the constitutionality of the entire confinement program, though it did hold that the War Relocation Authority had no power to confine or parole conditionally persons of undoubted loyalty.

His discussion of what constituted loyalty in that opinion is a moving one:

Loyalty is a matter of the heart and mind, not of race, creed, or color. He who is loyal is by definition not a spy or a saboteur. When the power to detain is derived from the power to protect the war effort against espionage and sabotage, detention which has no relationship to that objective is unauthorized.[67]

Despite this salve to his conscience, he and the majority of his brethren on the Court had, in permitting the internment in the first place, upheld what many civil libertarians regard as one of the most disgraceful actions in American history.

As evidenced throughout this discussion of Douglas's case opinions, his support of the war effort was firm, consistent, and the controlling feature of his jurisprudence. Once the war had ended, however, he quickly shifted to a position that advocated the broadest range of judicial review. This was clearly illustrated in a series of Selective Service classification cases that came to the Court during the closing phase of the war.[68] Douglas's most significant decision in that area was his majority opinion in the 1946 case, *Estep* v. *United States*.[69] In that case, two Jehovah's Witnesses challenged their draft classification on the grounds that the law did not provide for review of local draft-board classifications, leaving them with no judicial recourse.

Motivated by his concern about freedom of conscience, Douglas did not hesitate to overcome the wording of the law, which stated that the decision of the local board was final. Douglas, in contrast, held that congressional silence about judicial review would not be regarded as decisive. As he said:

... the question whether judicial review will be provided where Congress is silent depends on the whole setting of the particular statute and the scheme of regulation which is adopted. ... We cannot readily infer that Congress departed so far from the traditional concepts of a fair trial when it made the actions of the local boards "final" as to provide that a citizen of this country should go to jail for not obeying an unlawful order of an administrative agency.[70]

The assertion of judicial review as a check on arbitrary administrative power in the *Estep* case stands in marked contrast to Douglas's willingness to defer to the army's judgment in the *Hirabayashi* and *Korematsu* cases in the war years. The American victory in the war and the death of his close friend Franklin D. Roosevelt in the spring of 1945 removed the two major reasons for his subordination of personal civil liberties to governmental authority. Douglas would never again find himself caught on the horns of the dilemma that the wartime situation created for him.

His postwar case opinions and his off-the-bench legal writings would be marked by a consistent defense of civil liberties. His decision in the *Estep* case marks the beginning of a significant transition in his attitude regarding individual rights and the powers of government. He moved quickly to a position that defended First Amendment freedoms in the face of what many of his fellow justices felt were compelling reasons to restrict their scope. His postwar legal writings clearly record this aspect of his experience.

CHAPTER 3

The Shaping of the Wilderness Mind

THE postwar years witnessed an explosion of literary activity on Douglas's part. In addition to his two autobiographical volumes and some 800 Supreme Court opinions that he authored between 1946 and his retirement in 1975, he poured out speeches, articles, and books on civil liberties, conservation and wilderness preservation, and foreign policy, the three major topics that appealed most strongly to his restless, searching mind. His writing on these three major topics illustrated the continuing close connection between his experiences, beliefs, and writing.

I   The Celebration of Nature

Many scholars insist that Douglas's writings on wilderness values rank along with those on civil liberties as expressions of his fundamental beliefs.[1] There is a great deal of evidence in his extensive writings on nature, ecology, and conservation that would substantiate this view. His proposal that legal protections be extended to wilderness areas just as they had been to members of minorities and his outspoken advocacy of conservation reveal the intensity of his feelings on this subject. In this area, his writing served him well as a means of publicizing his beliefs.

Nature appears in Douglas's writing in its multidimensional complexity. He writes with clarity about its roles as teacher, friend, enemy, emotional catharsis, mystery, and, above all, something that can help man regain perspective on his place in the earth's environment. Though he lovingly describes its beauty, individuality, and diversity, he sees its brutal, demanding aspects as well. His own early experiences convinced him that nature challenged men to rise above their limitations and taught them how to live with their fears.[2]

Thus, whether he is taking his reader through a mountain canyon or on a visit to a favorite trout stream through his formidable descriptive powers and undisputed understanding of the ways of nature, Douglas has a message. The wilderness must be preserved! The blend of this advocacy with his personal adventures in the outdoors gives Douglas an appealing way to get his message across. It lends authenticity to his discussions of the problems confronting those seeking to preserve our wilderness heritage.[3]

Douglas's subsequent exposure to the writings of John Muir and Aldo Leopold and his extensive citation of them in his writings indicate that their ideas reinforced what he had learned by experience. They strengthened his desire to immerse himself in the wonders of nature. Like them, he came to see man's proper place in the universe as within instead of above the natural order of things.[4]

His reputation as an antibusiness activist came as much from his advocacy of the wilderness ethic as it did from his behavior on the SEC and the Supreme Court. Douglas was not a doctrinaire anticapitalist. He possessed a different set of values, one that rejected the hypocritical American attitude toward wilderness that praised its virtues while destroying it in the name of progress.

II   Of Men and Mountains: *The Seminal Work*

Douglas's love affair with nature proved to be a lasting one. It began during his childhood in the Pacific Northwest in a time of personal crisis for him. His 1950 autobiographical work, *Of Men and Mountains*, presents the best explanation of the causes of his deep attachment to the outdoors. It is a proper starting point for those seeking understanding of the essential assumptions in this aspect of Douglas's writings and the literary techniques he used to advocate them. It described the experiences shaping his devotion to the wilderness-conservation ethic. *Of Men and Mountains* is another example of the close ties between his personal experiences and his writing and illustrates the persistence of the values he formed early in life.

Most of those who reviewed *Of Men and Mountains* agreed that it is a clearly written volume marked by a personal, anecdotal, reflective style. It is a book about adventure and also an autobiographical statement. Above all, it is his own explanation of the crucial relationship between his wilderness experience and the shaping of his personality.

Douglas was certainly not the first or most famous of a large number of Americans whose attitude toward life was shaped by close contact with nature. Few, however, were more profoundly influenced by it than he. Writing in the foreword of *Of Men and Mountains,* he said in reference to the continuing attraction of the rugged mountain wilderness areas of the Pacific Northwest: "Here man can find deep solitude, and under conditions of grandeur that are startling he can come to know both himself and God" (p. ix).[5] The work is also philosophical in the sense that it illustrates the discoveries Douglas made about the meaning of life.

He summarized the chief lesson of his experiences in the mountains as follows: "I learned early that the richness of life is found in adventure. . . . But man is not ready for adventure unless he is rid of fear. For fear confines him and limits his scope" (p. x). His boyhood experiences had a lasting effect on his adult life.

His opening chapter, "The Cascades," set the mood for the entire book. He recalled how often in the midst of a monotonous case argument before the Supreme Court he would refresh himself spiritually and emotionally by reaching back into memories of his experiences in the mountain wilderness. In so doing, he presented a sharply contrasting picture of the drabness and pressure of urban life juxtaposed to the beauties of the Cascades. One of the best illustrations of his use of the flashback-contrast technique appeared in his account of how as a homesick young man he was living in a one-room walkup in New York City where the only plant he could see outside was a potted geranium. As he recalled: "In the poverty of that view the memories of the Cascades would come flooding back" (pp. 8–9). The beauty and detail of the description that followed was a testimony to his fondness for the mountains.

The first two chapters described the events of his early childhood. They revealed the events that took place after his arrival in Yakima, his father's death, his family's poverty, his attack of polio, and his resentment at being teased about his withered legs. Interspersed in his narration are hints of his attraction to the mountains and a moving description of the solace that he received from viewing the dominating presence of Mount Adams at his father's funeral. The two chapters really set the scene for the discussion of his increasing involvement with the mountain wilderness that followed. They also revealed Douglas's sensitive nature and his great sense of self-determination to overcome his physical handicap and the unintentional pressures to accept his disability as permanent created by his oversolicitous mother.

Chapters 3 to 7 contain superb descriptions of how Douglas rebuilt the shriveled muscles in his legs and his own self-confidence by taking increasingly longer hikes into the foothills and mountains around his home in Yakima. The chapters are well-balanced descriptions of how the recovery of strength in his legs increased his sense of self-reliance and his awareness of the wonders of the mountain wilderness where he walked. As he said when recounting the first time he walked twenty-five miles with a thirty-pound pack in one day: "I had conquered my doubts. So far as my legs were concerned, I knew that I was now free to roam these mountains at will" (p. 84). Triumph over his disability opened the way for other experiences. Descriptions of the way that these shaped his attitude toward life constitute the rest of the book.

Four chapters of the work are character sketches of men who lived their lives in the mountains—an anonymous Yakima Indian, a sheepherder, Jack Nelson (the gatekeeper of a wilderness reservoir), and Roy Schaeffer (a mountain guide). Each in his own way taught Douglas something about the value of life. The Indian taught him that a man could only be himself. Once he accepted that fact, he never lost his capacity to know his strength as well as his limitations.

The irony that he saw in the hunger for news of the outside world in the sheepherder made Douglas aware in the summer of 1914 of his patriotic responsibility and the larger lesson that one never escaped such demands. Jack Nelson taught Douglas that a mastery of the details of nature could bring harmony and peace of mind to life. Roy Schaeffer, on the other hand, taught Douglas the skills necessary to lead a full adventurous life in the mountains. All four of the men represented aspects of life in the mountains that Douglas admired and took unto himself. They symbolized the soundness and sincerity created in people by the mountain experience. Douglas derived great pleasure from the place he felt he had earned among such men.

That pleasure is best exemplified in the chapter "A Full Heart." The bulk of the chapter is a description of a daylong fishing trip he made through snow to Green Lake in the Wallowas. His description of the scene when he stopped at an icy brook to clean the trout he had just caught in the lake exemplifies his effective use of natural details to explain his first true appreciation of the scene's full glory:

Ahead of the grass were the buttercups. The meadow was golden with them in the late sun. There were spots of star moss on some of the rotten tree trunks. Hellebore, its leaves all furled in conical shape, was beginning to poke its head out of the ground . . . . (p. 196)

He was at home in the mountains because he knew them intimately.

Douglas also used *Of Men and Mountains* to illustrate the therapeutic effects of wilderness on humans. Recalling the time when he and a friend were stranded on a mountaintop in the midst of a northeaster gale, he said: "As I stood in the cold gale peering into the steep canyons, the froth of life seemed to blow away" (p. 210). To him, nature was the great leveler.

Douglas also drew valuable lessons from the brutal side of nature. In the chapter "Snow Hole" he related how he and some friends were caught in a blizzard and forced to survive by burrowing down into the snow beneath the snug of a fallen tree. While there, he came to the realization that: "When man holes up in snow, he returns to earth in a subtle way. . . . In a deep hollow of the snow, man returns to the womb of the earth to live. . . . He escapes the reality of the world and lowers the tempo of his own life" (p. 290). He was certain that such experiences not only taught him self-reliance but gave him a deepened sense of introspection.

Turning to the question of what one could gain from conquering high peaks, he brushed aside the explanation that it was merely a form of exercise. It was, he insisted, a spiritual experience, one where the individual tested the limits of his endurance. As proof of the spiritual effect, he cited a long list of authors whose writings supported his point. Little wonder that a number of the professional politicians in the Democratic party argued against the selection of Douglas as President Roosevelt's running mate in 1944 on the grounds that he acted too much like a boy scout.[6]

The final chapter in *Of Men and Mountains* is a description of his 1948 climb of Mount Kloochman in the Cascades, a peak he had first climbed as a fifteen-year-old youth. After describing his second climb, he used flashback to his initial climb to show how he had overcome panic during a close brush with death. It makes a particularly exciting climax to a book about adventures in the mountains.

Douglas, of course, told the story for other reasons related to the principal theme of his book. To him, Mount Kloochman symbolized the kind of challenge that had pushed mankind to the greatest triumphs. Challenge was thus the central theme in Douglas's philosophy.

After citing Arnold Toynbee's argument that the growth of society was the successful response to challenge, he discussed the implications of his philosophy for the troubled American society that he observed in 1950. Listing a number of the most powerful challenges confronting Americans, he argued that their solutions would require men who had lost the fear of living dangerously. Such were the kinds of men created by the challenges of the mountain wilderness. He was convinced that he was one of them.

Though Douglas was to write numerous articles and several more books in defense of wilderness values none of these approached *Of Men and Mountains* in terms of literary quality. It is a beautifully integrated volume that tells its story well and leaves the reader with a genuine sense of understanding about the importance of wilderness values in Douglas's personality development. Though his subsequent works stated his case for wilderness preservation well, with the use of the same mixture of descriptive material and philosophic arguments employed in *Of Men and Mountains*, Douglas's increasing concern about conservation and ecology brought a more strident, pleading quality to his later works. They also suffered from the haste with which they were written.[7]

III   *The Sharpening Focus*

Douglas's attachment to nature and its impact on his personality were also evident in his numerous articles on the outdoors in the 1950s.[8] In these he began to bring his specific beliefs about the wilderness-conservation ethic into sharper focus in the context of descriptions of his adventures in different wilderness areas. As his awareness of the dangers of technologically related pollution grew, so did the militancy of his position. As he said: "We deal with values that no dollars can measure."[9]

That concern, and the more fully developed critiques resulting from them, did not mean, however, that Douglas abandoned his formidable powers of description. This was readily apparent in his two wilderness books published in 1960 and 1961. Each was an account of his journey through a major wilderness area. Each reflected his continued successful integration of his personal experiences and his conservationist ethic.

The first of the two, *My Wilderness: The Pacific West*, is a descriptive celebration of his experiences in such wild areas as the Brooks Range in Alaska, Pacific Coast beaches, the Middle Fork of the Salmon River, the Olympic Mountains, and Douglas's beloved Willowa Mountains.[10] Taking up where he left off in *Of Men and Mountains*, he developed his narrative as a combination of personal anecdotal observations, natural and social history, and his beliefs on conservation. His mastery of the details of both the animate and inanimate aspects of nature is apparent throughout this work. This is true whether he is describing the place of the Arctic squid in the fragile ecosystem of the Far North or discussing the impact of the damming up of the Middle Fork of the Salmon River. The major theme of the work is clear: wilderness areas should be left as undisturbed as possible.

Already Douglas showed signs of moving toward what later became his advocacy of formal legal rights for wilderness areas. He spoke with approval of the great conservationist Aldo Leopold's remark: "The chance to find a pasque-flower is a right as inalienable as free speech."[11] Douglas's preoccupation with preservation runs through all of his writings on conservation. It was a view that brought him sharp criticism from those who sought to maximize public access to outdoor areas.

Douglas reiterated the belief in the superiority of wilderness values over those of the machine age that he had presented ten years previously in *Of Men and Mountains*. Citing an Indian student's comment on how soft Americans had become because of their dependence on machines, he argued that though civilization could be built around machines, it was doubtful whether a meaningful life could result from such a life-style. Nature, on the other hand, held out the possibility of renewing man's faith in himself, thus preserving his freedom from the mastery of the machine. Nature, in contrast to technology, presented a challenge that enhanced human, individual values.

The depth of Douglas's love for the mountains of his native Pacific Northwest and his desire to preserve their beauty are portrayed in the concluding paragraph of *My Wilderness: The Pacific West*:

This day Lightning and I were still in sunshine when the sun left the valley. Now the shadow passed us on its way up. The meadows at my feet were no longer sharp in detail. They took on an air of mystery. Then above me came the sweetest song I know. Audubon's hermit thrush sang over and over again. Its music is to me a haunting melody. It means the Wallowas, and lengthening shadows, and a sanctuary that greedy man must never destroy.[12]

What Douglas cherished here was something far beyond the realm of material values. To him it was the basis of peace of mind. He was defending the preservation of what had become an important part of himself.

Destruction of the wilderness was something that Douglas took personally. As he observed while viewing a high meadow in the Cascades: ". . . an emptiness in life comes with the destruction of wilderness; that a fullness of life follows when one comes on intimate terms with woods and peaks and meadows."[13] He saw no middle ground when it came to its preservation. His persistent condemnations of road-building into or near wilderness areas must be understood from this perspective.

Douglas thus summarized the forces threatening wilderness in *My Wilderness: The Pacific West* and its 1961 sequel, *My Wilderness: East to Katahdin*. Using the same format as in the former, he described his jaunts through wilderness areas east of the Mississippi.[14] Douglas failed, however, to articulate much in the way of a positive program to preserve them. Nevertheless, both of the wilderness volumes made it clear that he felt the situation was at the point of crisis, something Douglas liked to define as a situation containing elements of both danger and opportunity. They served to awaken the American people to the challenges confronting them in the realm of conservation. What was needed, he concluded, was a positive comprehensive program, one that would assure the place of wilderness in American life. This thinking led him eventually to conclude that wilderness preservation would require a formal bill of rights.

Like the great naturalist John Muir, whom Douglas first read as a boy, his was an attitude built out of intimacy with the western wilderness. In addition to his frequent references to Muir in his *My Wilderness: The Pacific West* and in subsequent works, Douglas published a children's biography, *Muir of the Mountains*, in 1961, a clearly written work with numerous anecdotes about Muir's younger years.[15] Douglas described the long developmental process that made John Muir our most effective public land conservationist. Drawing extensively on his knowledge of Muir's writings and his longstanding interest in the naturalist's contributions to wilderness preservation, Douglas used the volume as a means of educating young readers in the conservation ethic.

He used the last chapter to describe how Muir came to the conclusion that man's role on earth was ". . . not to destroy: it is to protect and conserve all living things." He acknowledged Muir's important role in making conservation ". . . a powerful, positive force in our national life."[16] The book reveals much about Douglas's preferences in heroes and the depth of his devotion to the wilderness ethic.

IV *Wilderness-Rights Evangelism*

Douglas's most comprehensive advocacy of the conservation–land-use ethic came in his 1965 work, *A Wilderness Bill of Rights*, a typical Douglas book in terms of its use of material developed in earlier writings and its approach. It represents his answer to the challenges confronting those who would preserve our wilderness areas. His proposed solution was a controversial one premised on a unique legal hypothesis that received enthusiastic support from wilderness preservation groups and sharp criticism from those who hoped to gain more access to wilderness lands.[17]

His was a view that emphasized the high priority that the conservation–land-use ethic commanded in his scale of personal values and his perception of the threat to it posed by modern technology. Douglas never lost his sense of gratitude about the significant role his wilderness experience had played in shaping his character. He was certain that the preservation of crucial aspects of the American character depended on our ability to preserve our wilderness areas.

A Wilderness Bill of Rights is divided into four sections and an appendix summarizing major acts of Congress in the conservation field. He used the two opening chapters to compare and contrast the values associated with technology with those associated with wilderness. He left no doubt as to where his own sympathies lay.

His first chapter, "Sewage, Automobiles, Population, and the Rights of Man," is a discussion of the forces leading to what he regarded as the desecration of wilderness areas. Citing the press of commercial interests, motorized recreationists, and a growing population, he painted a pessimistic picture of how these combined to create unrelenting pressures against the remaining wilderness areas in the country. The foremost enemy to Douglas was "our whole technological society" (pp. 3, 10–13).[18]

To illustrate the nature of the enemy, he cited a number of the by-products of our technology and their effects on ecology. Sewage and industrial waste, he noted, had either destroyed or were in the process of destroying such waters as Lake Tahoe, Lake Erie, and the Mississippi River. Nor were these wastes the only cause of water pollution. He described the erosion and silting caused by bulldozers and careless farming methods. To these he added the damage done by the excessive use of synthetic detergents and the impact of temperature-increasing power-plant generators.

Turning to the earth, he argued that the most destructive force at work in our forests and prairies was road-building. Roads into our parks and wilderness areas were the causes of the increased access that ruined their natural beauty. Douglas rejected the argument that those who opposed such access were the rich, the exclusive, and the young. He pointed out with pride that he and other elderly Americans hiked and backpacked regularly. Citing the July 1963 Forest Service brochure, "Backpacking the National Forest," he proceeded to catalog the virtues of backpacking.

The problem, Douglas insisted, was to find a way to get more Americans to see the values of hiking and packing when powerful forces were pulling them in another direction. "The road is the main culprit, and it often has the demanding voice of a majority of the people behind it" (pp. 22–23). Such an approach would lead to a pattern of more people with more cars overwhelming the remaining wilderness areas unless some use limitations were created.

Regarding the problems of creating such limits in a democratic society, Douglas admitted the difficulty of the wilderness exponents' position. He illustrated how they could easily be condemned as elitist or as opponents of growth and progress, positions distinctly un-American. Douglas argued, however, that the defenders of wilderness advocated another set of values that were also distinctly American.

He reminded his readers that our Constitution protected minority rights. The exponents of wilderness were a minority. Observing that there was no constitutionally valid guarantee that the 36.5 million acres of wilderness under federal control would be preserved, Douglas ended his first chapter by calling for a Wilderness Bill of Rights.[19] Douglas was convinced that man must not lose his sense of place in the natural order of things in the universe.

He then defined wilderness values and the reasons they were worth preserving by raising and answering three questions about them: "What are the wilderness values that this technological age is destroying? What wilderness values do we want to preserve? How important are they in terms of American civilization?" (p. 28). His answers to those questions presented a powerful confession of faith in the wilderness ethic.

Douglas noted with approval Congress's firm four-point definition of what constituted "wilderness" in the Wilderness Act. Its true meaning, though, went beyond the formal definition in the act. To him, "Wilderness is the earth before any of its wildness has been reduced or subtracted" (p. 29). It was something whose true value far exceeded the material value of the resources it contained. Like Thoreau, Douglas took his stand on romantic-humanist grounds.

Drawing first on his vast knowledge of history, Douglas began his assessment of the worth of wilderness. He pointed out that it was the backdrop for the saga of early American history, that it had served both as an "inexhaustible woodlot" and as a source of great inspiration. It had, in short, done much to shape both the material and spiritual aspects of our heritage.

Wilderness also reinforced the individuality that Douglas valued so highly. It provided a means of escaping the stereotyped existence and patterns of conformity created by our technology. Man could sense ". . . the endless wonder and excitement of nature's flair for individuality rather than conformity" (p. 31). It gave man a chance to develop perspective about his place in the universe.

Douglas utilized excerpts from the renowned conservationist Aldo Leopold's *Round River* to exemplify the ". . . lessons in time and in the interdependence of all life" gained from contact with the wilderness (p. 31).[20] Citing such oft-shunned areas as the great Dismal Swamp of Virginia and North Carolina and the bog of northwestern Pennsylvania as examples, he described how they were formed and the close harmony of their wildlife with their peculiar physical characteristics. He expressed concern lest the balance in them be upset by civilization.

He also saw the therapeutic value of contact with wilderness. It provided the means to reduce the tension created by the sounds and stresses of civilization. The lists of witnesses he marshaled to prove his point included Thoreau, Wordsworth, Muir, and Leopold, all of whom had personally experienced the healing effects of nature on their troubled minds.

Douglas's faith in the virtues of wilderness went even further. He saw its teaching potential as a form of living library, as one, however, that was in grave danger. Repeating Aldo Leopold and Charles Elton's arguments that the stability of a wilderness community depended on the extent of diversity within it, Douglas warned that such activities as bulldozing and the use of pesticides threatened this diversity. He noted with sadness that the needs of the wilderness were subordinated to a more powerful value, that of national growth.

To counter this, Douglas proposed the development of what he called the conservation ethic. He utilized the definition of it developed by Leopold in his *A Sand Country Almanac: With Essays on Conservation from Round River*: "A thing is right when it tends to preserve the integrity, stability, and beauty of the biotic community. It is wrong when it tends otherwise" (p. 37). The development of such an ethic would require striking changes in the attitudes of many Americans about the importance of conservation.

Douglas then discussed what would have to be done to achieve the creation of the conservation ethic. His initial suggestion was a call for education in conservation values beginning in the early years. It was his hope that an early start would offset the present land-use exploitation ethic currently dominating American thought. As a further means of presenting the conservation view, he urged that biologists, botanists, and ornithologists be placed on land-use planning agencies. Next he called for the development of legal techniques that could be used to head off land developers when they threatened wild areas. His final suggestion was that those interested in conservation try to make it a civic cause and to develop a united front against those who threatened the wilderness areas. The publicity and debate over ecology in the past decade indicate that his final suggestion has been at least partially realized.

After a long chapter surveying the wilderness and recreational resources available in America and how they were currently being mishandled, he turned to what he felt should be the chief ingredients in a Wilderness Bill of Rights. In a final chapter, one comprising nearly half of the work, he developed a more precise description of the specific legal protections to be included in such an approach.

Among the major points that he emphasized was a more restrictive definition of multiple use of wilderness areas to assure their survival. Though he saw it as a pragmatic approach when properly administered, he opposed its use as a cover for various pressure groups to gain their economic ends, something he referred to as ". . . little more than private enterprise engaged in boondoggling on the public domain" (p. 95). The critical questions, he realized, centered on who made the decisions on use and what priorities they used.

Douglas's mistrust of bureaucracy was evident in his second point. He called for congressional rather than more easily modified administrative designations of such areas. His aversion to bureaucratic decisions was based on observations of their harmful results. Public hearings were not automatically extended to questions relating to public property under the Federal Administrative Procedures Act. The potential for destruction of wilderness under unsupervised bureaucratic discretion convinced him that public hearings procedures should be applied to all aspects of land-use policy.

He also touched upon the difficulties encountered by conservation groups who attempted to publicize their side of the story. The tax-exempt status needed to collect funds was denied them because it is not granted to groups carrying on propaganda or influencing legislation. That provision of the IRS Code put the conservationists at a special disadvantage vis-à-vis the exploiters of public lands who could write off their advertising as a necessary and reasonable business expense.

Other important specifics in Douglas's version of a Wilderness Bill of Rights included severe restrictions on fencing public lands, motorized vehicles, boats, and aircraft, mining claims, industrial waste dumping, and damming of wild rivers and wetlands. His discussion was replete with references to specific areas and the current state of both legislation and policy with regard to them.

As in his early writings on conservation, Douglas expressed concern for the lack of safeguards against indiscriminate highway building. He sharply criticized the Commerce Department's Bureau of Public Roads "... whose ear is not tuned to conservation needs ..." (pp. 147–48). He condemned its road planners who stressed the quickest and cheapest ways to build highways. He called for statutory requirements that the Bureau of Public Roads conserve natural wonders even if it added to the cost of construction.

Douglas was certain his proposed Bill of Rights would fail unless accompanied by the creation of a new land-use ethic, one by which Americans learned "... to live with the land, not off the land" (p. 150). His use of Aldo Leopold's words from A Sand County Almanac underscored the influence of his thinking on Douglas's approach. Leopold articulated beautifully what Douglas believed about the proper relationship between man and nature (p. 151).

The changed attitude toward land use would also require other basic changes. One of these, dealing with the impact of chemicals on the biotic community, was a matter of critical concern to

Douglas. Referring to Rachel Carson's *Silent Spring* (1962), he called for strict regulation of predator control programs and pesticides because of their harmful effects on the environment. His concern here was based on his view of man as part of instead of something above ecology.

Douglas capped his discussion of his proposed Wilderness Bill of Rights by calling for the creation of a new federal Office of Conservation. He cited the "vast medley" of agencies such as the Army Corps of Engineers and the Bureau of Land Management whose actions affected conservation. His proposed office would represent the public interest in shaping the broader policies underlining the exercise of their functions. It would provide a means of controlling the bureaucratic discretion that he regarded as so inimical to wilderness interests.

It was not Douglas's intention to create another layer of bureaucracy. Yet, the office was necessary because ". . . we do need one that gives the President an overriding value judgment on whether the sacrifice or loss of conservation values in this project or that proposal is worthy of our civilization" (p. 173). His equation of wilderness rights with fundamental civil rights would thus be reinforced by a government agency.

A Wilderness Bill of Rights marked the culmination of Douglas's defense of the conservation–land-use ethic. It revealed his mastery of the law and literature on that subject. Though he certainly held expansive, idealized views of the virtues associated with wilderness preservation, they were deeply rooted in his own experiences. Moreover, he was brutally realistic and statistically very convincing in his depiction of the threats that technology posed for the shrinking areas of wilderness in the United States and the dangers associated with the multiple use concept that had long dominated our conservation policies.

As in other aspects of his writing, the challenge motif was very much in evidence in this work. He left his reader with a sense of foreboding about the implications of current trends and policies. So also, as in his other topics, he presented a counterplan that called for a radical departure from current policies. He did not underestimate the difficulties associated with overcoming the opposition to the idea of a Wilderness Bill of Rights.

His belief that the concept of wilderness preservation could be given statutory protection like the rights of minorities was especially significant. It represented his attempt to codify those values that he held so dear. Formal legal status would give the advocates of wilderness preservation a powerful, permanent weapon.

A *Wilderness Bill of Rights* is Douglas's most fully developed exposition of the land-use ethic. As such, it presented an excellent picture of the basic assumptions underlying the preservationist position in the continuing bitter debate over the best ways to use public recreation lands. The tenacity with which Douglas defended his position is indicative of the depth of his attachment to those values.

V *Warnings of Disaster*

In 1967 Douglas tried to reinforce the point that he had made in *A Wilderness Bill of Rights* by focusing on the tremendous pressure that was causing the destruction of wilderness areas. He did this in *Farewell to Texas: A Vanishing Wilderness* by examining the situation in the wilderness areas of one state.[21] Written as the first volume in McGraw-Hill's American Wilderness Series, of which Douglas was the general editor, the work is marked by a return to the personal, anecdotal style that characterized his earlier "My Wilderness" volumes and his travel-adventure works. The result, then, was a much more readable volume than *A Wilderness Bill of Rights*, one that reinforced the message of that work quite effectively.

Farewell to Texas is a narration of Douglas's trips through the remaining wilderness areas in Texas. In it he used general history, natural history, and character vignettes about the inhabitants of the wilderness areas to illustrate the natural grandeur that they possess. As one reviewer has noted, his descriptive powers were such that he succeeded in giving his readers a real feeling for the areas described.[22] The sense of appreciation he evoked for the natural attractions of Texas made it easier for him to plead the case for conservation and preservation.

Some sense of Douglas's passion for the Texas wilderness can be seen in the descriptions of his visits to the different areas. His appreciation even extended to those regarded as most inhospitable to man. In reference to his journey to the canyons of the Rio Grande he said:

I always leave the Rio Grande reluctantly. The swiftness of the rapids, the beauty of the canyon walls, the solitude of the chasm are too quickly passed. The urge is to return again and again in order to have a more intimate look, to explore the high caves, to search out the wealth of agates and fossils that these canyons reveal. It is hostile country in a sense, not even the water being safe to drink. The bushes mostly have spines; the walls are precipitous; the rocks are either dangerously brittle or dangerously sharp; the great slide in Santa Elena is terrifying. But the call of adventure is strong, and those who run these canyons once will return, drawn by the twin magnets of beauty and danger (pp. 90–91).[23]

The effective transmission of his personal experiences to his reader is a crucial element in his writing.

Douglas's devotion to contrapuntal writing is also evident throughout the book. In the preface, for example, he praised the growth of the conservation movement in Texas but hastened to stress the threat to wilderness by adding that there were forces at work ". . . to reduce large portions of that state to the status of Naboth's vineyard," whose beauty made it the target of King Ahab's desire and Jezebel's conspiracy (p. vii).[24]

Douglas's list of those contributing to the destruction of the natural beauty of Texas was a long one. It included public utilities with the power of eminent domain, federal agencies—especially the Army Corps of Engineers with its dam policies—stockmen who overgrazed, lumber barons who clearcut, vandals, oil companies, poachers, and ranchers who used pesticides indiscriminately. He proceeded to develop a discussion of the effects of those "modern Ahabs" on Texas wild lands in the midst of his discussion of their beauty.

The resulting effect was a striking contrast between what was, what is, and what will be. He hoped to raise Texans to the "heroic action" needed to save the remaining fragments of Texas wilderness. The challenge was particularly great in Texas because so much of its wild area was on private rather than public lands and thus less subject to use regulation.

His invective spares nothing that threatens wild areas. One of the best examples of his fervor in *Farewell to Texas* was his attack on one of his favorite targets, the effects of dams on Texas wild areas:

Dams, dams, dams—they are the plague of Texas. They are a modern form of pork-barrel grants. Other sources of power are plentiful. When dams are needed for flood control, they could be placed high on the tributaries. They not only silt in early and become useless; they often produce ugly shore lines of mud and debris; they destroy forever rich

bottom lands; and they are wiping out the chronicles of early man that give
Texas some of its richest culture. (p. 117)

He makes frequent references to such writers as J. Frank Dobie,
John C. Duval, and many others who knew their home state well.
Mentioning these devoted Texans throughout the work clearly
reveals his close association with the leading advocates of wilderness
preservation in that state. It also indicates that he backed his own
observations with the knowledge of experts ranging from academics
to inhabitants of wilderness areas. Such remarks were used to
reinforce rather than to substitute for what Douglas had actually
observed in his journeys through the wilderness areas of Texas.

Douglas concluded sadly that time and private economic groups
were working against those who were laboring to save the remaining
Texas wilderness. His charge that Texans had not yet entered the
twentieth century in terms of conservation practices was a devastat-
ing one. He urged all-out support of continued federal and state
efforts to create more parks such as the Big Bend National Park. His
concluding plea to save the remnants of Texas wilderness for future
generations was one of his most eloquent in a long series of such
statements. As in his *A Wilderness Bill of Rights*, he emphasized the
critical need for reeducation in the conservation ethic, a task that
would prove most difficult given the popularity of the acquisitive,
materialistic side of American culture.

The disturbing process he characterized in Texas was only the tip
of the iceberg as far as Douglas was concerned. His increasing alarm
about the costs of technology and our material culture created a
growing interest in the dangers of pollution. As with his ideas on
other aspects of the environment, it soon appeared in his writing.
Once again, he argued that man must act before it was too late, not
just for the sake of wilderness but before the earth was too damaged
to support human life.

Douglas's last book before his death on conservation and the
environment, *The Three Hundred Year War: A Chronicle of
Ecological Disaster*, was published in 1972.[25] Though his goal is the
same as in *Farewell to Texas*, his approach is quite different. What
he tried to accomplish in the earlier volume by focusing on one
state, he tries to achieve in *The Three Hundred Year War* through
a more generalized approach. In contrast to his narrated tour of wild
areas in the former, *The Three Hundred Year War* is an expository
essay brimming with references to scientific authorities designed to

lend credence to his frightening message. The central point of his argument is his increasing doubt about man's ability to reverse the pattern of ecological devastation caused by the uses of technology. He develops this thesis in his initial chapter and uses the next dozen chapters to discuss the kinds of pollution created by a society that is dominated by faith in its technology and an absence of an ecological ethic. His final chapter is a discussion of the types of political action available to those seeking to stop the movement towards disaster. The result is a somber volume in which Douglas's overriding interest in ecology shines through.

The general causal forces that Douglas saw behind the continuing rape of the earth and growing ecological disaster were the twin gods of technology and materialism, forces that had played critical roles in the shaping of Western culture. As he notes: "Technology and the profit motive have carried us far down the road to disaster. It is indeed a desperate race to institute preventive controls that will save the ecosystem" (p. 168).[26] More specifically, he condemns big business and government bureaucracy whose policies combined to fulfill the notion of progress inherent in the technological and materialistic world around us. He indicts the former for evading environmental pollution regulations in pursuit of maximum profits and the latter for permitting such things to happen through the confusion, ineptitude, and acquiescence that typify the operation of Parkinson's Law in the self-perpetuating federal bureaucracy.

The problem, he insists, cannot be laid just at the door of business and bureaucracy. The American people also share the blame:

As a people we have no ecological ethic. We talk much about Law and Order and we mean it when we say that burglaries, street crimes, holdups and the like must cease. But in a deeper sense we have a basic disrespect of law—unless the law restrains the other group, not our own. (p. 10)

Finding a means of changing this attitude is a crucial part of Douglas's approach.

He insists that the major problem to be overcome relates to the sacrosanctity of the doctrine of economic growth in Western culture. Lest Douglas's message be regarded as an attack on capitalism, it should be noted that he makes numerous critical references in *The Three Hundred Year War* to the ecological sins of the Soviet Union. Relying heavily on the writings of Aldo Leopold, Barry Commoner, Jacques Cousteau, and others as proof of the harmful effects of the blind pursuit of unrestricted economic growth, Douglas lays the groundwork for an alternative approach.

Questioning the traditional equation of no economic growth with stagnation and decay, he points out how the fragile ecology of the earth will no longer permit such a policy. Instead, he urges that Americans become aware of their place in an enlarged community that includes, as Leopold said, "... soils, waters, plants, and animals, or collectively, the land" (p. 18). Such an awareness would necessitate the development of a standard of growth based less on output and more on improvement of the quality of life.

As the means to stem the headlong rush toward disaster, Douglas discusses the question of gaining standing to sue in cases defending the interest of environment. Though he notes some progress toward acceptance of that technique, he cautions against reliance on courts that are oriented toward the status quo and easily influenced by "industrial lawyers." Ultimately more effective, he maintains, would be an approach based on making conservation a Messianic religion, one that motivated its believers to move beyond the public relations approach to one based on political action. Chief among the goals of this activism should be a more human, less exploitative land-use ethic, one based on ecological considerations.

Douglas, reflecting his beliefs in the paramount importance of political decisions, urges conservationists and ecologists to unite and carry out a number of specific actions. These include insisting that all heads of federal agencies dealing with conservation be subject to presidential appointment and Senate confirmation so their attitude toward environmental problems can be accurately gauged, requiring that public hearings be held on all major conservation decisions to insure that the environmentalist position be heard, and imposing high fines and prison sentences for those violating pollution laws.

Douglas also confronts head-on the argument that antipollution laws mean a loss of jobs. All industries, he argues, should be held to high antipollution standards. Such a requirement would greatly reduce the obstructive capabilities of those who threaten to move to states and communities that are more lenient about pollution controls. Government should compensate and retrain workers who lose jobs because of such actions, and those unemployed could be rehired for environmentally useful projects.

The Three Hundred Year War is a fitting, though sad, summation of Douglas's advocacy of ecological sanity, the conservation–land-use ethic, and wilderness preservation. It is a last concerted effort to get his fellow Americans to see what he saw so clearly. It is, like so much of his writing, advocacy of his point of view, a position that made him a hero to ecologists and the bête noire of many federal bureaucrats and members of the American business community. Recent events such as the Love Canal pollution problem and the accident at the Three Mile Island nuclear plant seem to bear out his arguments about the immensity of the dangers posed by technological pollution.

Evidencing his well-established abhorrence of bureaucratic ineptitude, he urges citizens to short-circuit the potential harm it causes by getting involved in self-help ecology projects at the local and state level. The question is: "Can saving the environment become as holy a cause as making a fast buck?" (p. 196). It is essential for Americans to apply his proposed conservation ethic.

He concludes sadly that efforts thus far on the environmental front have largely been public relations gestures and that the earth's ecology is worse off than a decade ago. Embittered by our involvement in Vietnam because of its diversive effects on the ecological crisis, he asserts bitterly: "Our priorities have been an overseas war, not the Three Hundred Year War at home" (p. 199). Change would require a conversion to activism on the part of Americans. He closes with a moving request that his fellow Americans accept the respect of the Sioux Indians for ". . . the goodness and the beauty and the strangeness of the greening earth, the only mother" (p. 200).[27]

Douglas's hopes struggled fiercely with his pessimism in *The Three Hundred Year War*. He left his readers with the impression that his mind knew what his heart could not accept. These later writings on ecology reflect growing doubt about man's ability to overcome the challenge posed by technological pollution.

CHAPTER 4

World Affairs: Problems and Solutions

WILLIAM O. Douglas was a perceptive student of world affairs long before he achieved popularity as author of a series of travel-adventure books on "strange lands and friendly people." He traced his interest in world affairs to the family discussions connected with Presbyterian missionary efforts that he heard as a child. His subsequent advocacy of the exportation of democratic practices owed much to the evangelical missionary impulse though the content of the latter was far different from the former.[1]

It is also true that Douglas, like so many of his fellow New Dealers, was drawn toward world affairs by the rise of Fascism and the eventual involvement of the United States in World War II.[2] He readily accepted the idea that the United States was involved in a later version of Woodrow Wilson's earlier crusade to make the world safe for democracy.[3] So likewise, in numerous postwar speeches, articles, and books on world affairs, he expressed his continuing concern about the threat to democracy posed by the Cold War and its pervasive impact on American foreign policy. His firsthand observations of the turbulent conditions in the emerging nations of Asia and Africa during the postwar years provided him with a factual basis for what became his increasingly critical attitude toward official American foreign policy.[4]

Douglas's discussion of America's role in world affairs reveals an interaction between deeply held fundamental assumptions and his growing awareness of the changing realities of the international situation that leads him ultimately to a strong advocacy of democratic values within the framework of a world peace through world law position as the means of averting a nuclear holocaust.[5] The twin goals of preserving peace and growing room for democracy played major roles in shaping Douglas's frame of reference and his proposed solutions to the challenges confronting the United States in the postwar world.

76

I   *The Basic Assumptions*

As in other aspects of his writing, Douglas's books on foreign policy and world affairs are usually summations of ideas and experiences he had already articulated in speeches and shorter articles. In 1948 Richard J. Walsh collected a number of Douglas's speeches and articles written during his first nine years on the bench and published them under the title *Being an American.* Walsh selected excerpts from Douglas's thinking and placed them in four topical divisions: "The American Idea," "The Public Service," "Problems of Our Times," and "Postwar Horizons." Whether or not the volume was intended as a campaign document for an attempt at the presidential nomination, as one critic suggested, the seven selections in the last section present an excellent index to the dominant ideas in his approach to world affairs in the early postwar period. Nearly all of the fundamental assumptions in those writings as well as the style used to present them were to typify Douglas's treatment of world affairs throughout his public career.

Douglas's initial postwar comments reflected the persistence of his wartime patriotism and idealism. They are more generalized and less replete with concrete examples and analysis than his later writings on this topic. Pride in the western tradition with its vital ideals as exemplified by Christian and Jeffersonian thought forms the basis of his early discussions. He warned that Americans must be prepared to compete in the world, while at the same time avoiding the political immaturity that created social and moral default and led to war. He urged an approach to foreign policy based on a combination of ideals and beliefs ("the imaginative mind" and "quick practicality"). He was particularly interested in Americans pursuing the ideal of justice, even if it meant refusing to defend the status quo.

The need for an active role in world affairs, one that emphasized the necessity of America facing up to reality, is a persistent theme running through all of Douglas's writings. He exhorts Americans to exercise world leadership while at the same time practicing caution about commiting ourselves to policies before carefully considering their consequences. As he put it: "Let us hesitate to act until we know the truth. But then let us act decisively; otherwise, the very refusal to act becomes a policy—the most self-defeating policy in the world" (p. 167).[6] The idea of passivity in world affairs was alien to Douglas's mind.

The necessity for facing challenges was also deeply rooted in this aspect of Douglas's thought. It played a significant role in shaping his view of what was required of Americans in world affairs. He urged his fellow citizens to avoid settling for mere economic security. Americans, he said, must never lose their desire to reach for improved spiritual and social conditions. Douglas's preoccupation with the importance of facing challenges represented a transfer of attitudes from the realm of his personal experience to that of national affairs.

Also evident in *Being an American* was his strong attachment to the need for some system of world government. He viewed the newly formed United Nations as a first step toward a world system of law, expressing hope that out of it would evolve the necessary institutions to control the nuclear instruments of mass destruction. This belief had its origins in his traditional legal realist principle that law could serve as an instrument of change and his confidence in man's ability to work out the means for his own survival.

His answer to the "isms" that he saw as the product of exploitation and suffering was the exportation of technical skills and democracy. His was not the blind adherence to an ideal like that which marked the attitudes of many Wilsonians earlier in this century. American assistance to the "underdeveloped" peoples, he insisted, ". . . entails some financial commitments; but it means not so much the export of dollars as the export of knowledge—know-how and program, technical skills, and the like" (p. 186). He envisioned the export of such things as largely the responsibility of private citizens through the efforts of social, religious, cultural, and economic associations. He argued that a nation that had carried the word of God to the remote corners of the earth could carry the dynamic elements of life in a democracy to the same places.

Another important theme in his writings on America's role in world affairs was his insistence that Americans come to understand the nature of communism. Douglas's extended treatment of that subject in *Being an American* was originally developed for an address that he gave at the University of Florida on March 22, 1948.[7] His initial treatment leaned toward the traditional Cold War assumption that the world Communist movement was well disciplined, under the control of Moscow, and striving for world domination. As proof, he suggested that liberals and conservatives alike read Joseph Stalin's *The Problems of Lenin and the Foundations of Leninism*.

The author then sought to develop his ideas about the nature of communism by drawing a series of contrasts between it and democracy. The first irreconcilable difference between the two systems, one that he saw as a great advantage for the free world, was the diversity in democracy. As he put it:

This rejection of absolutes, this freedom for experimentation mark the first basic and irreconcilable difference between the political philosophies of the totalitarian Right and the totalitarian Left on the one hand and the political philosophy of the democrats, on the other. (p. 190)

Communism, on the other hand, tolerated no views that challenged its dominant political-economic theory.

Douglas, with what was one of his favorite persuasive devices, made use of one of the Founding Fathers, James Madison, to illustrate the second irreconcilable difference. He cited Madison's call in *Notes on the Confederacy* for the construction of a government in which no interest had the power to impair the rights of others. Douglas saw the process of maintaining this balance in American society as a continuing struggle. He portrayed communism, on the other hand, as a government dominated not by a dictatorship of the proletariat, as Marxian doctrine held, but instead as one dominated by a "select political clique" that had arbitrarily declared class warfare as the central problem of the age (pp. 194–95).

The third and most significant difference that Douglas saw lay in the realm of political techniques. Citing civic genius as a characteristic of democracies, he used William James's definition of it as ". . . the habit of trained and disciplined good temper towards the opposite party when it fairly wins its inning" (p. 197). By contrast, the Communist Left has no room for such "accommodation and compromises." As proof, he cited Stalin's writings about use of the tactic of participating in democratic institutions prior to gaining control of and eventually destroying them.

Turning to the question of the proper means to meet the Communist menace, Douglas outlined what proved to be the basic approach that he maintained throughout his career. Not unexpectedly, it involved the United States seizing the initiative against its Communist foes. Emphasizing the importance of understanding Communist tactics, he called for ". . . a dynamic and vital political program on the democratic front" (p. 201).

He first argued the necessity of integrating domestic and foreign policy in his approach to the Communist question. He regarded the domestic aspect as the easier of the two. He called for an end to the use of smear tactics that branded all advocates of change and dissenters as Communists and for the development of a more effective democratic government. The former was important because it would lessen the false sense of fear permeating American society and the latter because it would effectively rebut the Communist argument that there are irreconcilable differences between classes in society. (The relation between Douglas's civil-libertarian ideas and the growing witch hunts of the Cold War years will be treated in the next chapter.)

Immensely more difficult, to Douglas, were the international aspects of the Communist challenge. Reiterating his belief that Alexis de Tocqueville's classic distinction between Anglo-American reliance on personal interests and the Russians' reliance on authority was still valid, he emphasized that the basic differences between Russia and the United States continued to be political ones. Douglas's definition of "political" here is a broad one that regards all nonmilitary action against the Russians as being in that category. Thus a foreign policy fashioned merely in terms of anticommunism would fail because it would ". . . do nothing to eliminate the conditions on which communism thrives" (p. 203). An effective policy would have to be one that reached the masses and strengthened the democratic forces rather than the reactionary elements in other nations. Douglas's subsequent travels in the Third World caused him to become even more insistent on this point.

He reminded his audience that much of the world was ". . . a serfdom of poverty and disease" that the Communists could easily exploit. He urged Americans to offer ". . . practical programs of social reconstruction" rather than merely verbalizing our ideals over Voice of America radio. The critical thing to remember, Douglas argued, was that the battle with communism ". . . will be won in the rice fields rather than on the battlefields" (p. 205). Thus there was need to support those with democratic values who could relate to the masses.

He closed his work by reminding his readers that: "Inexorable forces are sweeping the world. We are part of those forces, since we were among the first to kindle the spark of freedom" (p. 205). Douglas urged the United States to remember and exploit that link between its revolutionary past and the yearning and needs of the developing nations.

The treatment of foreign affairs in the speeches and articles reprinted in *Being an American* is the prototype of the entire Douglas approach to foreign policy. Though he did flirt briefly with the notion of a monolithic world Communist movement, his growing awareness of the uniqueness of Chinese communism caused him to surrender that idea very quickly in the early Cold War years. With that one exception, all of his books on world affairs that followed proved to be amplifications and refinements of his early position. They underscore both Douglas's confidence in his basic beliefs and the tenacity with which he defended them.

II   Travel and Adventure: Their Clarifying Effects

Much of the impetus for Douglas's increasingly critical stance on official American foreign policy came from his personal observations during a series of overseas journeys beginning in the late 1940s and continuing through the late 1950s. His passion for travel and adventure gave him the opportunity to view firsthand the impact of our foreign policies in the Near and Far East. He described his trips in a series of travel-adventure books published between 1951 and 1958: *Strange Lands and Friendly People; Beyond the High Himalayas* (1952); *North from Malaya: Adventure on Five Fronts* (1953); *Russian Journey* (1956); and *West of the Indus* (1958).

Written when Douglas was at the height of his ability to create narratives combining history with vivid anecdotal description and interesting personality characterization, the series of books are superb travelogues. They are also, however, vehicles for Douglas to relate the implications of his observations about America's role in world affairs.[8] In addition to the comments interspersed with his discussions of geography, history, and personal anecdotes, the author concludes each of his travel-adventure works with an extended discussion of that topic.

Quite expectedly, the Cold War preoccupation with the growth of communism looms large in his travel-adventure books, but the response that Douglas propounded to combat it is something far different from the traditional practice of containment. It signifies Douglas's attempt to transcend the negative mentality that he felt the Cold War cast on American policy. The result is an imposing body of interpretation supported by concrete, interesting examples of the problems confronted by the developing nations and the inadequacy of the American response to them.

The hypothesis that emerges from this series of books is marked with elements of both pessimism and optimism. Its central argument is that American foreign policy was failing in its objective to check communism because it was based on erroneous premises and assumptions. His comments reflect his grave doubt that reliance on guns, dollars, and technology would assure American security and the stability of the areas emerging from colonialism. American ignorance of the profound changes in the world and the nature of communism lay at the root of her policy problems.

The first, and in many ways the best, of Douglas's travel-adventure books, *Strange Lands and Friendly People,* was published in 1951. It was an account of two trips taken in the summers of 1949 and 1950 to Greece, Cyprus, Israel, Lebanon, Syria, Iraq, Iran, Pakistan, and India. Douglas's dedication of the work to his mother, ". . . who once knew poverty in the Middle East meaning of the word," suggests much about the overriding impression that he received from his journey.[9]

His childhood experiences gave him a strong empathy for the common people he saw during his travels. All of his travel works reveal acceptance of what his life experience had taught him, that poverty did not destroy the dignity of mankind. So likewise did his announced intention to illustrate ". . . through the medium of personal experiences, the main stresses and strains in the area" reveal the approach used in all of his travel-adventure works (p. xii).[10]

Douglas initiates his discussion of what he had learned from his journeys with the remark that his return from the villages of Asia had left him profoundly disturbed. He is convinced that neither Americans nor Asians understand each other. The basic thing that Americans would have to understand, according to Douglas, is that a revolution was occurring in Asia, one, though exploited by communism, whose fundamental causes went far deeper. As he says: *"The revolutionaries are hungry men who have been exploited from time out of mind. This is the century of their awakening and mobilization"* (p. 315).

Reaching back as usual into American history for an analogy, Douglas observes that the causes of discontent in Asia reminded him of the list of grievances American colonists had accumulated against Britain by 1776. Though different in their specifics, the Asian grievances were of critical importance as agents of revolutionary causation. Such diverse forces as lack of medical care and schools and desire for land reform tied to modern farming techniques merged with a growing sense of nationalism to fan the fires of revolution.

Our critical failure in Asia, according to Douglas, has been that the United States has never addressed itself to the problems cited above. He sharply criticizes our support of reactionary regimes merely on the grounds that they are anti-Communist. He argues that this mistook an effect (communism) for a cause of the changes sweeping Asia. It was one of the tragic effects of a foreign policy built too narrowly on the singular precept of anticommunism.

What solution does Douglas suggest? First and foremost, he felt the United States should ". . . throw its weight on the side of the honest, liberal elements which can be found in every country" (p. 319). If such a course had been followed, he asserted, China would not have gone Communist. He then lists four major errors in American policy toward Asia and expresses confidence that they could yet be overcome. The four include our negative state of mind as seen in our preoccupation with anticommunism, too much reliance on our military for policy formulation, too much subservience to British policies in the Middle East, and the belief that dollars can stop communism.

By contrast, the Asian policy that Douglas prefers includes surrender of the idea that the world could be shaped in the image of the West, the realization of the idea that tensions in Asia run deeper than communism, the sharing of our food surplus, and the sending of education missions to build goodwill. More generally, Americans must realize that Asian problems would take a long time to resolve and any political program that we develop for Asia should be based on that assumption.

Douglas's final point is a warning that Americans must drop our sense of superiority based on a high standard of living and replace it with a vision of what other people and their leaders aspire to in the future. Warning that democracy could not be imposed from above, he emphasizes that it would have to come from within the peoples of the developing nations.

In 1956 Douglas published *Russian Journey*, an account of his visit to the Central Asian Republics of the Soviet Union. Utilizing the personal anecdotal approach that he had developed in his previous three travel-adventure books, he presents a fascinating picture of a diverse number of aspects of Soviet law, politics, economics, and culture that he observed during his 1955 visit. The result was an impressive collection of insights about life in the Soviet

Union from the perspective of an interested, open-minded, though not entirely uncritical, observer.[11]

In a concluding chapter entitled "The New Russian Strategy," Douglas presents his general conclusions about what he had observed should shape American policy toward the Soviet Union. They are the Russian people's desire for peace, the belief of the Kremlin leadership in the ultimate victory of communism, and Russia's proximity to her southern neighbors that gives her great advantages in the contest for their people's minds. Peaceful coexistence, Douglas warns, would create a political challenge the like of which the United States had never experienced before in world affairs.

Douglas was convinced that the Russian desire for peace was a genuine one based on the realization among its people that a higher standard of living could come only with the avoidance of war. This feeling was reinforced by the new leadership in the Soviet Union, a group he called a "talented elite" that did not want to see its status destroyed by war. Such a drive for peace, he cautioned, did not mean that the ultimate aim of communism had changed.

This situation had forced a change of tactics on the part of the Soviet Union. The result was a new Russian strategy even more dangerous than the old Stalinist one based on conspiracy. Russia's new "open" policy in the realm of world politics would require an imaginative American response. This was true because: "The new Russian strategy is more disarming. It is to use oats, not a whip, to drive the horses, as an old Russian proverb counsels" (p. 233).[12] The Soviet strategy then relied on the use of economic and military aid combined with selective trade policies and diplomacy to advertise the superiority of the Communist way of life.

Douglas also warns that the Soviet missionary attitude toward communism would also play an important role in their new politics. He points out that Americans have never really understood the "nature" of the relationship between Communist Russia and the peoples of other lands. As he puts it: "Though it is a conspiracy, it is cast in terms of brotherhood. It is the old, old theme of one for all and all for one. It has for many the same universal appeal as Thomas Jefferson's creed" (p. 237). It had universal appeal and presented a powerful rallying cry for the oppressed, something that gave the Russians a considerable advantage in a contest where so many of those involved were poor and exploited.

What antidotes did Douglas think would be effective against the revamped Russian strategy? He begins by repeating his long-held belief about the primacy of dealing with communism with political action. He calls for affirmative, flexible programs that, for example, make distinctions between Socialists and Communists. Most critical, though, he insists, would be our approach to relations with the Soviet Union. His prediction that the deep antagonisms between Russia and the United States would mellow in time was new. It would become increasingly important in his subsequent writings on Soviet-American relations. He pointed to the emergence of the new Soviet leadership and an ultimate Russian-American dependence on each other in the face of Asian instability and eventual nuclear capacity in that region.

The problem confronting America is its immediate response. Douglas presents two choices. The first is the continuance of the present policy of military preparedness accompanied by a stepped-up version of our international economic program. The second involves the creation of a political truce accompanied by disarmament, friendship, and nonaggression. He chooses the latter alternative because it seemed to promise the greatest chance for mutual security and an end to the arms race. He closes by expressing optimism about the powerful influence that the rights associated with democracy could play in peaceful competition with the Soviet Union: "They give the West a great advantage in the competition— if we will only think in terms of people, their fears, their needs, and their dreams" (p. 244). Douglas never relinquished his faith in the power of democratic ideals. His increasingly critical perception of American foreign policy grew out of his belief that American policies in the Cold War were frustrating the use of our most effective weapon, our heritage of freedom.

The last of Douglas's travel-adventure books, *West of the Indus*, was an account of his 7,000-mile auto trip from Karachi, Pakistan, to Istanbul, Turkey, in the summer of 1957.[13] In it Douglas stuck to the same anecdotal-picaresque approach that he had used so effectively in his earlier travel-adventure works. As one reviewer noted:

Without being unaware of the scenery, the travelers were more concerned with meeting the people of the countries through which they traveled and deliberately chose the by-ways that led to villages and the more isolated areas.[14]

The discussion of American reactions to the situation in the countries that Douglas traversed is decidedly less optimistic than in his earlier travel books. Instead of concluding his book as he had his previous travel-adventure volumes with a specific chapter on America's role in the parts of the world he had explored, Douglas uses an account of his meeting with a party of American tourists as a vehicle for expressing his criticism. In talking to them, Douglas learned that ". . . they were intrigued with Asia but full of misgivings" because they had been conditioned to think that the only way to fight communism was with guns and that the revolutions sweeping through Asia could be repressed.

To Douglas, the American tourists symbolized in microcosm the tragedy of America's view of Asia:

> They were fascinated by the colors and mysticism of Asia but nervous about its stench and its dirt. They wanted to enjoy in Asia the American standard of living. That meant that they would see Asia from luxurious hotels, not from the highways and byways. They would go to teas in Embassies and see something of the social whirl of the capitals. But they would never get close enough to the villages to feel the heartbeat of the people.[15]

Sadly, and with a sense of foreboding, he concluded that the American tourists whom he met symbolized the ". . . growing gulf between America and the East, the gulf that threatens to leave us in lonely isolation."[16]

III   America Challenged: *Criticism in Full Bloom*

The maturation of Douglas's growing concern about the wisdom of American foreign policy is recorded in the last half of his brief 1960 book, *America Challenged*.[17] The work is the printed version of two lectures he gave at Princeton University in March 1960. Like many other books that were revised versions of his lectures, it was characterized by the brevity, clarity, and succinctness that were the hallmarks of Douglas's writing.[18]

The chapter entitled "The Nation and the World" is a hard-hitting, frank assessment of the situation confronting the United States in world affairs and his suggestions about the way the problems related to it could best be overcome. Utilizing a geopolitical frame of reference, Douglas opened with the blunt assertion that the world situation was largely beyond the power of the United States to shape according to its own wishes. Therefore, he called for a policy based on negotiation rather than confrontation.

Douglas made it clear that he had not abandoned his "contest-challenge" frame of reference regarding the Soviet Union. He explained how Russian proximity to Asia gave her many advantages in the contest for the hearts and minds of the peoples of that continent. The Russian efforts included the creation in central Asia of an economic showplace, the acceptance of thousands of students from the developing lands, and the effective use of her "Gold Reserve," technicians trained in the language and culture of the lands where they were sent in large numbers to aid in development. The real contest the Russians aimed at winning through these methods, Douglas emphasized, because of mass illiteracy and poverty, was control of the elite in those developing nations who were struggling with such problems.

Using one of his favorite analogies, that the Chinese symbol for crisis is a combination of those for danger and opportunity, Douglas said that the situation America found herself in at mid-century was neither bright nor hopeless. What was needed, he insisted, was a reversal of our Marshall Plan approach with its overreliance on money and guns as solutions to all of our favorite foreign-policy problems. Though that approach had been successful in Western Europe after World War II because of the existence of viable democracy, representative institutions, and an industrial economy, it did not fit conditions in Asia or Africa. As in his realist approach to law, new situations created the need for new ideas in foreign policy.

Restating one of the earlier themes, Douglas reminded his audience that the basic problem of survival was political and not military. He then turned to the kind of policies the United States should implement in the threatening world surrounding it. His first suggestion was one that became increasingly important in his thinking: the United States should lead the world community in the outlawing of nuclear power for military purposes. In one key passage he stated:

We cannot as a people sanction the use of any instrument either for experimentation or for war which makes the soft trade winds, the great refreshing gales out of the west, and the gentle rains the agents of death. We cannot stand mute while the air is polluted by explosions, endangering people on all the continents. (pp. 44–45)[19]

He was convinced that the United States would lose moral leadership in the family of nations if it continued to develop nuclear weapons. The step that Douglas urged was the development of international controls. That, however, did not go far enough. Convinced that nations would still resort to atomic weapons in the event of war, the critical necessity was the prevention of war. So the need to give nations options short of massive retaliation became increasingly important in world affairs.

Along with that conclusion, Douglas reiterated another of his basic ideas, the need for a system of world law capable of managing the inevitable conflicts and disagreements that arise as a result of human variety. But Douglas was no blind idealist on this matter. He cited with regret the paucity of cases that were taken to the International Court of Justice as an example of how much work was yet to be done. As he said: "We cannot expect a world system of law suddenly to appear full-blown and adequate for all contingencies" (p. 47). His point was that there must be a series of small steps in that direction such as the development of special devices to adjudicate controversies and to administer such things as nuclear energy.

Lest anyone dismiss his arguments as naive, Douglas hastened to emphasize that only "dreamers" would believe Communist intentions could be altered by the politics of disarmament. Preserving military capability and cooperation among the democratic nations in the world community was of critical importance. "Coexistence," to Douglas, did not mean the end of conflict and competition between two sharply contrasting ways of life but rather the use of negotiation to "restrict the areas of conflict" thus giving changing circumstances a chance to have their way. As an example, he cited the mutual interest that the Russians shared with the United States regarding the stabilization of Asia in light of the growing power of China.

Douglas used the rest of *America Challenged* to discuss the implications of a number of aspects of America's role in world affairs and to suggest ways American policy could be made more effective. Starting with economics, Douglas used growth rate and allocation of resource statistics to warn Americans that the Russians used far less of their gross national product for consumption than we did. This left the Russians with more of their resources to advance their aims in the contest for the minds of the peoples in developing lands.

He suggested two things to offset this Soviet advantage: "(1) keep strong militarily and be able to carry our share of aid to underdeveloped nations; (2) expand greatly in our services to our own people" (p. 54). Quoting Walter Lippmann's arguments, Douglas urged that greater amounts of national wealth be committed to public purposes thus accelerating our chances of competing with the Soviets in education and foreign aid. Douglas's concern about too much emphasis on consumption of material things, a major theme in his wilderness writings, is used here to support a pragmatic political argument.

Addressing himself specifically to the needs of the underdeveloped nations, Douglas defined the essential problems that they faced and the things Americans could do to help them. His basic starting point was that most of the peoples of the world lived in primitive agricultural societies at what we regard as a subsistence level. The struggle of these peoples, even with their willingness to industrialize, would take a long time to raise their living standards. It was a problem that would have to be approached with patience.

The world food crisis was an area where Douglas saw possibilities for American help in education and cooperation to insure expanding supplies. The wise, humane use of our food surpluses in the face of exploding birthrates could be an advantage in the continuing political contest with the Russians. Douglas totally rejected the idea that food should be used, as some have recently suggested, as a coercive weapon. Remembering an impression from his travels through lands threatened with famine, he said: "We never can afford to let loose the hatred that hungry people have for him who shuts the door of the granary in their faces" (p. 60). Food would instead be a bridge of goodwill between the United States and the hungry peoples in the developing world.

Douglas also condemned the massive amounts of sophisticated weapons the United States sent to such poverty-stricken countries as Ethiopia where the need was for literacy programs, hospitals, and schools. He admitted, though, that his own reaction was an "oversimplification" because the most crucial problems in the emerging nations were not entirely economic. Instead, he pointed out: "They start with the need to develop viable societies along democratic lines" (p. 64). It is at this point that he emphasized the value of the American system of checks and balances with its restraints of majorities and protections for minorities as an especially useful example.

Much of America's contribution should be in the realm of educational assistance, something Douglas defined as ". . . creating the power within the people of a nation to solve their own poblems [sic]" (p. 62). Asians and Africans should be encouraged by the thousands to study in America. So likewise, in a remark that seemed to foreshadow President John F. Kennedy's creation of the Peace Corps, he urged that thousands of our teachers be sent abroad to build "the close intellectual nexus" with those who will rule the new nations of Asia and Africa. To accomplish this, we would have to overcome the reluctance of thousands of our people to master the language, history, and traditions of the nations of the world. Unlike the subsequent Peace Corps effort that did emerge as a government agency, Douglas, like President Dwight D. Eisenhower, called for a people-to-people effort undertaken by private groups instead of the government. This would avoid the stigma of foreign intervention in countries newly emerged from colonialism.

Douglas's final suggestion was aimed at strengthening the democratic nations' commercial ties. Reaching back into American economic history, Douglas pointed out that much of American economic growth was the result of the common market-free trade situation that evolved in this country. Such an approach, he thought, would work well among the democratic nations of the world if they would take time and patience to bring it about. Permitting the emerging nations to join such a common market would allow them to attract the basic investment capital needed for development. The result, according to Douglas, would be: "They will quickly develop bonds and patterns of cooperative action which will make for a unity that no amount of money and no amount of speeches can create" (p. 70). Economic cooperation went hand in hand with and strengthened political cooperation.

These then were the suggestions that Douglas believed would prove effective against the threat of communism. A sound American response to the world situation would eventually bring about opportunities for cooperation with the Soviet Union as it developed more pluralist tendencies. As Douglas said: "Time moves on and creates new conditions" (p. 73). The changes, he warned, would only be effective if Americans sloughed off the complacency, mediocrity, and intolerance that he saw as impairing efforts to exert their leadership in world affairs. His conclusion points to his awareness of the critical relationship between domestic and foreign policy. *America Challenged* is undoubtedly Douglas's seminal work on foreign policy. Written in the period of disillusionment and inaction at the end of the Eisenhower presidency, it is a work that reflects the maturation of his critical approach to foreign affairs.

IV   Douglas's Plan: The Rejection of the Status Quo

Douglas subsequently wrote four books and numerous pamphlets, articles, and speeches on world affairs all aimed at amplifying his proposed solutions to the challenges to security that Americans

faced in an increasingly hostile world. All typically were characterized by the mixture of realism and idealism that had long been at
the center of his approach to foreign policy, all saw the need for the
departure from traditional approaches to foreign policy, all called
upon Americans to surrender some of their biases about their role in
the world for the sake of a more internationalist perspective, and all
sought peaceful solutions to problems in a world threatened by
nuclear holocaust. They clearly illustrate the preeminent place that
the challenge motif occupied in his thought and writings.

In 1962 Douglas published *Democracy's Manifesto*.[20] Asserting
that the United States had been on the defensive against international communism for too long, Douglas used the volume to present
"A *counter plan* of grand design . . . lest the promises of the
communists appear to the masses as the only alternative that is
tolerable" (p. v).[21] The result was a typically succinct volume based
on personal observations written from the same "we're behind and
here's why" perspective that Douglas presented in *America Challenged* but one containing a more specific discussion of ways to
overcome the errors in American foreign policies.

His central thesis was that our intense preoccupation with anticommunism had caused us to extend financial and military aid to
the reactionary elements who were, in turn, attempting to repress
the evolving revolution against colonialism and feudalism occurring
in the developing world. He insisted that such an approach played
right into Communist hands because it failed to get at such critical
problems as landlordism, usury, and economic stagnation that
fanned the fires of discontent.

According to Douglas, security would come from two things: first,
great power nonaggression agreements—including banishment of
guerrilla warfare; and second, pacts both to defend and to promote
regional interests. He then discussed the possibilities for such pacts
in Asia, the Mid-East, and Europe, reminding his readers, as in past
works, that the ideological contest would still continue. Such an
approach on our part, however, he predicted, would lead to striking
changes in Eastern Europe, the Soviet Union, and in China,
especially in the growth of "unorthodoxy" in those regimes.

Douglas devoted a large part of this brief work to a discussion of
his most cherished goal in world affairs, the creation of a peaceful
world filled with free societies. As a first step, he urged the end of
support of those elements in the status quo that prevented the
emerging nations from creating a free society like ours. To do this,

he said, the villages must be changed from places of squalor, disease, and illness to healthy communities. Ways would have to be found to give foreign aid with conditions that assured its being used for crucial village development. Education, improved farm technology, and training in self-government, the basics Douglas advocated, would be the agents of revolution in the world.

Douglas preached the virtue of patience in his approach to foreign policy, a patience reinforced with idealism. He shared Abraham Lincoln's faith in the applicability of the principles in the Declaration of Independence to all mankind. While American democracy could not be exported in its literal forms, ". . . the ideas which it represents are contagious and enduring" (p. 47). It was by its example that the United States could present the concept of a free society as an option to feudalism and communism. That Douglas could believe this in the face of world conditions was proof of his faith in the potency of grassroots democracy.

V   Advocacy of World Law

Detailed discussion of another important aspect of his thinking on world affairs appeared in his long pamphlet *The Rule of Law in World Affairs* (1961), which summarized his views on world law as he had presented them at a meeting at the Center for the Study of Democratic Institutions, Santa Barbara, California. It was a detailed explanation of a number of the points he had made in the patient advocacy of a world law system in speeches and articles since the end of World War II.

By his own admission, Douglas's approach to world law owed much to the ideas presented by Grenville Clark and Louis Sohn in their major book, *World Peace through World Law* (1958). He shared their gradualist approach to the creation of such a system. Douglas's devotion to the idea of world law had its origins in one of his fundamental beliefs, his faith in the rule of law as a cornerstone of American liberty.

Brushing aside the doubts of cynics, Douglas rejected the traditional argument that such a system would require a sovereign superstate to enforce world law. Instead, he urged the creation of a system of law that would shape cooperative conditions rather than coerce obedience. One immediate incentive, heretofore missing, that he saw for the use of the cooperative approach was the growth of the destructive capacity of modern weapons with their potential for nuclear accidents.

As evidence of his "bit by bit" approach, he cited examples of a number of forces pushing nations toward the creation of world law. A major one, according to Douglas, was the activity of the United Nations.[22] Especially important was the sense of security the emerging nations got from their participation in UN programs as they emerged from colonialism.

Injecting a sense of realism into his work, Douglas admitted that there were tremendous gaps in customs, practices, and mores—that it was wrong to ". . . think of the world as if it was made in our image."[23] This view, though, was offset in part because insecurity in the world was creating pressure for a rule of law. Douglas concluded that the common grounds for initiating a system of world law would be narrow and selective. Essential to it would be the outlawing of aggressive war. He believed that the proliferation of nuclear technology made war so dangerous as to be obsolete.

VI   *The Federalist Corollary*

The other crucial part of Douglas's approach to world law was the idea of federalism. His thinking on this subject was governed by the belief that the system of government developed in the United States with its flexibility and balancing of state, local, and national interests could be applied successfully to the international situation. Douglas's most detailed discussion of world federalism came in the final chapter of his volume, *The Anatomy of Liberty: The Rights of Man Without Force,* published in 1963,[24] prior to the disillusionment he experienced as a result of the Kennedy and King assassinations, our deepening involvement in Vietnam, and the tragic domestic confrontations of the middle and late 1960s.

Douglas optimistically predicted that compacts, whether initiated for defense or economic cooperation, would grow and eventually broaden into such things as common markets because they were the most effective regional problem solvers. Such regional solutions, however, would require further readjustments in American foreign policy, including a shift away from creating military alliances and client states on the borders of Russia and China. His basic point that there would be few solutions to world problems that could be resolved by American military power alone has certainly been substantiated.

Douglas conceded that the formation of regional groupings raised problems as well as resolving them. Most important was the question of how the economic "have" nations like the United States, Russia, and those in Western Europe would accommodate their policies to the "have-nots."[25] He stressed the importance of not being so exclusively tied to one trade group as to injure the industrial attempts of the "have-nots" nations, where products would be cost expensive and thus in a less competitive position regarding our markets. Again, he leaves the reader with a sense that he is aware of the terribly complicated problems faced by anyone seeking to bring about basic change in a world fraught with the dangers of nuclear confrontation.

Douglas's next book-length study of world law, *Towards a Global Federalism*, was published in 1968.[26] Written in the midst of rancorous division over American involvement in Vietnam and the violent domestic confrontations that marked the mid-1960s, the volume is characterized by his pessimistic, and, in places, bitter treatment of American foreign policy. In his preface, he expressed skepticism about the ability of Americans of his generation to understand the book. This was true, he said, because Truman, Churchill, and Stalin had filled the world with so much suspicion and hatred, thus preventing his own generation from acting creatively. Instead, he aimed the book at those Americans under forty whom he felt would have the last clear chance to avoid nuclear destruction.

Though this book presents numerous arguments in favor of a consensus approach to peace through world federalism, its central theme is more specific. Douglas dwelt pessimistically on the crippling effects of American foreign policies on efforts to achieve that goal. In so doing, he revealed his belief that much of what the United States did was in error because of our fundamental misunderstanding of world realities.

He said that the cause of American failure was the fixation of our Washington bureaucracy on the notion that the best deterrent to communism is a strong middle class. Douglas argued that, unlike conditions in Europe, where the Marshall Plan had met success, the conditions to create such a class were missing in many of the developing lands. Thus the American attempt in Latin America had failed and the rich had gotten richer as the poor got poorer. American aid programs were thus based on an erroneous premise as far as the developing nations were concerned.

Douglas used his concluding chapter in *Towards a Global Federalism* to analyze the effects of ideology and racism on American foreign policy. Like the giant in *Gulliver's Travels*, he asserted,

America was being threatened "with impotence by pygmies."[27] In America's case, the pygmies were divided into two groups: one advocating racism and the other the Cold War. Together, they had made us "largely impotent" to deal with the immensity of international problems.

Turning first to the effects of the Cold War, Douglas charged that the mentality created by it had blinded us to the diversity in communism, drawn us into an arms race that made us captives of the military mentality, and created a dangerous pattern of conformity in American society. The result was that America had become paranoid and unable to reach cooperative solutions to world problems through diplomacy and law. To Douglas, the classic example of the bankruptcy of the American approach was our presence in Vietnam.[28]

The second of the two major paralyzing influences on America's foreign policy was racism. In describing its effects, Douglas said:

While the Cold War was largely responsible for our Vietnam venture, there was, as well, another powerful subconscious influence operating insidiously. For our domestic political philosophy has long rested on an unstated premise of white supremacy.[29]

He explained that despite our constitutional ideals, America had not escaped from the taint of racism and its corollary belief about the Yellow Peril. These deficiencies made it difficult for the United States to claim leadership in a racially diverse world.

He rejected the idea that the removal of our preoccupation with race and ideology would solve all of our foreign policy problems. But, he insisted, racism and poverty had, in short, caused many in the East and West to ". . . react to racial and ideological, rather than to human problems."[30] Douglas's approach to world affairs, his strong advocacy of world law, was an integral part of his essentially humanist philosophy.

VII   *Six Steps to Peace*

Douglas's last two books on world affairs were published in 1971 with the announced purpose of examining different aspects of dissent and rebellion in world affairs. Both *International Dissent: Six Steps Toward World Peace* and *Holocaust or Hemispheric Co-op: Cross Currents in Latin America* were extended treatments of the most important themes Douglas had developed in his previous writings on foreign policy. They contained strong statements of his belief in the need for a new approach to that subject. Each of the works reflects Douglas's continuing attachment to the idea that it would be necessary to create a new ethic of international responsibility before the critical issues dividing nations could be resolved.

Despite its title, *International Dissent* is a statement of Douglas's views about how to deal with the international tensions and disagreements that lead to war. Douglas used it to present his theses about the causes of wars and his ideas on their prevention. As he said: "This is a book about law, not law as it can be found in a library but law as it must be and will be *if* we are to avoid the nuclear holocaust."[31]

Rejecting the idea of unilateral solutions for international conflicts, he cited six alternative solutions to the use of force. Though uncertain of their results, he was convinced that they offered the most likely chances to avoid nuclear destruction. The remainder of *International Dissent* is a discussion of these propositions. They include the elimination of military alliances, abolition of all colonies, recognition of Red China, international control of the ocean floor, and economic assistance to developing nations.[32]

Douglas saved until last what he regarded as the most difficult to achieve of his propositions. It was critically important, he insisted, that the laws governing international relations focus on the elimination of war.

He posited some rules of international law in areas of critical need where he felt progress was possible. He was convinced that the first rule of law should be built on gaining consent to submit all boundary and territorial issues to international tribunals or agencies. His second called for a means of settling disputes over territorial and international waters. A third forbade the invasion of any nation by another. A fourth sought restrictions on the sale of armaments to developing nations. A fifth called for an agency to "exercise oversight" of growing environmental problems.

The final chapter of *International Dissent* is an apt summation of the conclusions Douglas drew from twenty-five years of observation and discourse on America's role in foreign affairs. His basic thesis was that disarmament could only come after ". . . comprehensive measures are taken to change the attitude of the Great Powers toward world problems."[33] Douglas cautioned that, because of competing ideologies, the world would never be free of struggle and conflict. Yet he insisted that

The new federalism would deal with conflicts between nations just as our own Supreme Court deals with conflicts between sovereign states. Internal disorder would be beyond its competence, unless that disorder spilled over into a neighboring state.[34]

A strong sense of awareness of the difficulties involved in the creation of a world legal system runs through Douglas's extensive writings on that subject.

He cautioned his readers that such things as the economic imperialism practiced by developed nations, subversion and sedition, and pressures for social change will not disappear. Yet, as he said: ". . . competition and consensus are part of the same dynamic process."[35] It was his hope that the fear of nuclear war would be the driving force behind the moral and ethical changes necessary to create cooperation in the realm of conflict resolution.

VIII   *The Cooperative Approach*

Douglas's last book on world affairs, *Holocaust or Hemispheric Co-op*, was his most extensive attempt to apply his principles of international cooperation to an underdeveloped region.[36] The result is a frank, factual book about the massive problems involved in developing United States–Latin American cooperation. Douglas's proposed solution was consistent with the proposed fundamental departures from traditional American policies that he had advocated in his previous writings on world affairs.

He used the prologue to argue that, although there had been much talk about hemispheric cooperation, little had been accomplished. As an example, he summarized the negative results of the eight years and $8 billion spent on the Alliance for Progress. The effort had left Latin America with an unfavorable balance of trade and increased barriers against its industrial products.

He used the first eight chapters to present a comprehensive survey of important aspects of life in Latin America. He included brief but knowledgeable discussions of the racial and cultural mixtures in that region, the interaction of nationalism, elitism, and modernization, the necessity of understanding the forces of popular change, and the role of the military and social elites. He leveled strong criticism at the practices of American industry in Latin America, particularly the way it placed its economy in the role of resource supplier and balance of payments debtor through our trade system.

Douglas's last three chapters present his ideas on the essentials of a whole new approach to the problems confronting Latin America. At its core was his proposal for the creation of a hemispheric co-op as the best means of overcoming the region's massive problems. He emphasized that five critical steps would be necessary to bring such a co-op into reality. These included a multilateral approach supervised by the United Nations, withdrawal of all military missions and aid, and creation of a Pan American educational satellite. To these proposals he added two specific economic suggestions: a village revolution based on land reform, increased food production, and population control, and the development of investment programs better suited to use the labor surpluses in the Latin economies.

As in all of his writings on world federalism, Douglas emphasized the problems standing in the way of the creation of a hemispheric co-op. Such obstacles as American opposition to Latin American neutrality, loss of our economic clients, the intensity of Latin American nationalism, and diversity in stages of development from country to country all posed great challenges. He felt that these could be overcome when the Latin American nations realized the tangible benefits they would gain from such a co-op.

Douglas used his epilogue to argue that the initial requirement for a successful hemispheric co-op was the same as that in many other aspects of American foreign policy. As he put it: "Only drastic changes in attitudes will make that possible."[37] With characteristic bluntness he reminded his audience that the American people did not have a happy, confident relationship wih the peoples south of the border. Quite to the contrary, history revealed that the American role was one of intervention in Latin affairs, too much support of the status quo, and economic alliances with the elite who controlled the governments and the military. Americans must be prepared, argued Douglas, to accept the revolutions and land reforms that will come, be prepared with ways to help the Latin Americans use their surplus of labor, and provide assistance in education and planning.

Douglas's advocacy of world peace through a system of world law and federalism grew apace with his fears of the danger of nuclear holocaust. The "bit by bit" approach he hoped would develop out of practice and experience left ample room for experimentation. So also did his support of world federalism with its corollary of regional federations and co-ops underscore his belief in an evolutionary, nonauthoritarian approach to world law. The frustration of his efforts to convince many Americans of the need for a new approach to foreign policy led to growing disillusionment on his part. The result was an increasingly critical perspective on American behavior in world affairs, especially the inability to approach adequately the question of achieving peace.

Douglas's writings on world affairs thus share one significant theme with his writing on other major topics: it was marked by his concern lest the United States succumb to the sense of fear that had once threatened to impair his own spirit. That fact explains much about the persistence and intensity of his critique of American foreign policy.

CHAPTER 5

Civil Liberties: The Balancing Approach

A NY attempt to do more than assess the general assumptions and cite selected examples of significant trends in Douglas's extensive legal writings and case opinions in a work of this size would border on the ridiculous. As discussed in the first chapter, Douglas made his mark as a legal scholar early in his career, publishing extensively in the highly technical field of corporate reorganization. From that period until ill health forced his retirement from the Supreme Court in 1975, he wrote numerous articles and several books on legal and judicial topics as well as some 1,200 case opinions during his tenure as a justice. Because of the massiveness of this aspect of his writing and the importance he attributed to it, it is an area that deserves treatment in any assessment of Douglas's contribution to the American literary tradition.

As with the other aspects of his writing, there are significant elements of growth and change in the evolution of Douglas's predominantly realist constitutional philosophy. This is especially true in his First Amendment civil-liberties opinions in which he started out with a balancing approach and shifted to an absolutist position. It is also important to remember that Douglas presented his constitutional philosophy in effective, clearly worded prose, going directly to the points he sought to make. This habit makes it easier to examine his approach to judging than that of many other judicial figures.

Because of the quantity of opinions associated with each aspect of his legal writings, selected significant Douglas case opinions and writings will be here divided into categories covering two chronological periods. The first, extending from 1945 through the mid-1950s, was the period when he used a balancing approach to First Amendment civil liberties. The second, extending from the mid-1950s to 1975, was the period when he advocated judicial absolutism. Douglas's case opinions and off-the-bench legal writings during each of the periods will be treated separately.

I   *Off-the-Bench Legal Realism: 1945–Mid-1950s*

One of the best examples of Douglas's continued adherence to the legal realist tenet that law had to reflect the changing realities of a society appeared in an address, "*Stare Decisis*," he presented to the New York City Bar on April 12, 1949.[1] In it Douglas described the growth of *stare decisis* and its relation to man's quest for security. Security, he pointed out, was not a static entity. Ironically, "The fact is that security can only be achieved through constant change, through the wise discarding of old ideas that have outlived their usefulness, and through the adapting of others to current facts."[2]

Douglas did not deny the value of uniformity and continuity in law, but recognized the problems caused by maintaining old practices in the face of new demands. He viewed judicial review as a process that played a dynamic role in a world of continuing change. As he often did, Douglas resorted to a historical example, in this case the importance of judicial interpretation of the meaning of the Fourteenth Amendment in American history. Douglas's treatment of *stare decisis* in his speech presented a clear example of how that principle was to him an inadequate approach to law, one that restricted the uses of law in a way that contradicted the activist nature of his personality.

To Douglas, the Cold War raised grave threats to American civil liberties and the judicial means available for their protection. During the first postwar decade, he authored many speeches and articles advocating strict adherence to the procedural guarantees of the American Constitution as a means of protecting individuals from the hysteria of the Cold War. An October 1947 address, "Procedural Safeguards in the Bill of Rights," typified his concern.[3] He used it to present what was to become a persistent theme in his discussion of civil liberties—that though they were marked by varying forms and objectives, totalitarian regimes all found excuses for the suppression of individual rights. Therefore, he cautioned: "We must be alert that we do not emulate totalitarian regimes by curtailing the press, by suppressing free speech, by persecuting a minority, whether racial or political."[4] That responsibility, he felt, was the special province of the bar.

Douglas's 1952 essay "The Black Silence of Fear" illustrated his growing concern about the effects of Cold War orthodoxy on freedom of expression in America. There Douglas reiterated his argument that the uniqueness of America was our tradition of civil liberties including the right to freedom of thought. He pointed with dismay at the impact of the Cold War on that aspect of American freedoms.

Fear has many manifestations. The Communist threat inside the country has been magnified and exalted far beyond its realities. Irresponsible talk by irresponsible people has fanned the flames of fear. . . . Once we could debate with impunity along a wide range of inquiry. . . . Now there is suspicion.[5]

The connection between Douglas's position here and his own experience with the conquest of personal fears is evident.

Douglas's continuing calls for procedural integrity in the face of growing pressure for orthodoxy revealed a search on his part for antidotes to the animus against freedom of expression caused by the fear of communism.[6] More significantly, they illustrated Douglas's growing doubts about the viability of the balancing approach for the protection of individual civil liberties. That discontent was one of the major causes that would eventually propel him toward First Amendment absolutism.

In 1948 Douglas discussed another crucial aspect of his judicial personality, his willingness to dissent sharply from his brethren on the Court, in an essay entitled, appropriately, "The Dissenting Opinion." It was a particularly relevant essay, given his frequent disagreements with the restraint-oriented majority of the Vinson Court. The result was an interesting example of the connection between his own beliefs and judicial behavior.

As he frequently did to make a point, Douglas resorted to contrast. Absolute certainty, he noted, was something possible and typical under totalitarian systems that refused to tolerate disagreement. In a democracy, Douglas argued, things were different. Citizens should not be surprised, then, when judges are divided on the deeper issues that divide society itself. Douglas turned to Charles Evans Hughes for a justification of this view of dissent:

A dissent in a court of last resort is an appeal to the brooding spirit of the law, to the intelligence of a future day, when a later decision may possibly correct the error into which the dissenting judge believes the court to have been betrayed.[7]

It was this perception of the high worth of the dissenter's function that Douglas carried with him into the postwar years.

Douglas published two books on legal subjects in the mid-1950s. The first, *An Almanac of Liberty* (1954), was the product of his growing interest in civil liberties and his desire to inform the American people about the difficult struggles that had accompanied their evolution.[8] The work is marked by the application of Douglas's anecdotal skills to an almanac format.

Selecting a significant occurrence that he felt advanced the cause of freedom for each date in a calendar year, Douglas presented several very brief excerpts and a few longer essays about what he regarded as the highlights of Anglo-American civil liberties. The selections were those he had written sporadically over a long period of time while studying questions about the evolution of American freedoms. The resulting mixture of British and American history with his own personal insights led to what one reviewer called a book of Douglas's ". . . pungent and cogent obiter dicta" on civil liberties.[9]

An Almanac of Liberty produced valuable insights about Douglas's conception of how civil liberties evolved and why they were so important. The unifying theme in the work is clear: civil liberties evolved out of a long period of struggle that continues to this day. His previously cited concern that procedural guarantees be honored despite pressures for shortcuts also appeared regularly in the selections. He reserved special praise for those who dared dissent and paid the price for the courage of their convictions.

Despite recurrent setbacks in the struggle surrounding the development of individual liberties, Douglas remained optimistic. Even the restrictive pressures of the Cold War era did not deter Douglas's belief that civil liberties would prevail if Americans remained true to their heritage of freedom. This aspect of Douglas's belief added to the thematic unity necessary to overcome the fragmentation inherent in the episodic organization of the work.

An Almanac of Liberty is a work that is best read slowly so that the full impact of its implication for those interested in contemporary civil liberties can be digested. The sense of ". . . down-to-earth realism and quiet sanity" that the reviewer Ralph H. Gabriel saw in the work combined with its simplicity of style to make it a most

readable volume. It was a firm defense of the value of civil liberties
at a time when they were gravely threatened by the passions
generated by fear of Communist subversion. Most importantly, the
work presented a clear picture of Douglas's conception of how basic
American liberties were formulated and how they must be cherished
and actively defended. The latter task he regarded as a challenge of
the highest order, one that would continue to demand much effort
from his fellow Americans.

Douglas's second legal book in the postwar period, *We the
Judges*, is an edited version of the Tagore Lectures that he gave at
the University of Calcutta in 1955.[10] As such, the work is an
explanation of the American constitutional system with comparative
remarks on its Indian counterpart. Because of its intended audience,
its language is simple and direct and its case analysis is presented in
nontechnical language. It is in typical Douglas style, full of his
personal comments on constitutional development and the judicial
process.

The work reveals Douglas's mastery of American and British
constitutional history. Each of its twelve chapters has three different
aspects: the growth of the American doctrines being discussed, a
comparison with the relevant Indian law and precedents, and a
discussion of Douglas's perception of the ideal democratic standard
for each specific right. It is in the treatment of the latter topic that
the flash points of Douglas's constitutional and judicial philosophy
are clearly illuminated. It is there that his preoccupation with
individual rights is most evident.

We the Judges is an important volume because it is full of
indicators about the state of Douglas's legal thinking as he approached the threshold of judicial absolutism in the mid–1950s. As
his explanation of the origins and use of the political questions
doctrine suggests, he believed in definite limits on the times when
judges should apply judicial restraint. To illustrate his point, he
criticized the Court's majority for their decisions in the *Colegrove* v.
Green and *South* v. *Peters* reapportionment cases: "Yet if dilution
of a vote on racial or religious grounds is a justiciable issue, it is
difficult to see why dilution through the unit system is not also in
the same category."[11] He saw great danger in too extensive an
abrogation of the judicial function.

If the judiciary bows to expediency and puts questions in a political rather
than in a justiciable category merely because they are troublesome or

embarrassing or pregnant with great emotion, then the judiciary has become a political instrument itself.[12]

There should be no excuses for running away from the responsibility to judge.

Douglas also expressed concern about the threats to civil liberties posed by some aspects of government practice in the 1950s. He sharply criticized the misuses of congressional investigations in his chapter on legislative prerogatives. Buttressing his argument with references to Erwin N. Griswold's *The Fifth Amendment Today* (1955), Walter Lippmann's *Essays in the Public Philosophy* (1955), Alan Barth's *Government by Investigation* (1951), and Telford Taylor's *Grand Inquisition* (1955), Douglas emphasized the threat to executive independence and personal civil liberties posed by overzealous members of congressional committees.

Though he admitted that the rights to ask a question and demand an answer are essential to the democratic process, he was not convinced that the investigatory function was boundless. As he stated:

While American courts have not spoken with finality on the reach of the investigative power, it is clear that the power being derived from the Constitution rises no higher than its source, and even in its limited sphere exists only insofar as it is congenial to other constitutional rights and guarantees.[13]

Caught in the paradox caused by his belief in the efficacy of the investigatory power and what had become its gross misuse, Douglas resorted to a balancing approach. It did not prove to be a permanent one.

His treatment of administrative agencies also illustrated his changing attitude toward them. Admitting that they were useful parts of the government hierarchy, he charged that such agencies had created new problems and abuses. Their critical flaw was the lack of what he had called for in his earlier discussion of administrative government: ". . . a high standard of the public service."[14] His strong sense of concern for individual freedom and his disappointment at the decline of idealism in government combined to stimulate what proved to be a strong animus against administrative excesses during the last two decades of his public career.

The final chapter of the work, "The Judiciary," is a thorough discussion of Douglas's own views about the duties and responsibilities of the judges. It is valuable for what it reveals about his approach to judging. In a manner loyal to his immersion in legal realism, Douglas argued that though the doctrine of *stare decisis* played an important role in private law it had little place in American constitutional law.

He used the closing paragraphs of the book to state his concerns about the threat posed by recent political developments to judicial independence and civil liberties. His primary fears concerned the development of unchecked bureaucratic and legislative power at the expense of the judiciary. Underlying Douglas's growing antipathy to legislative and administrative actions was his growing conviction that ". . . the realm of conscience should be placed beyond the reach of government." [15] The importance of procedural integrity as a shield for freedom of conscience was a central theme in Douglas's approach to civil liberties. He saw the process of judicial review as a critical element in the preservation of civil liberties, particularly freedom of conscience.

We the Judges contains much evidence of Douglas's increasing preoccupation with civil liberties. His case analysis and asides reveal his hope that the American and Indian constitutional systems would develop more effective tools to protect individual freedoms. The book suggests that he was actively searching for more effective means to protect individual freedoms than he had found in the balancing process that had dominated his approach up to that point in his career.

II   *The Proper Approach?*

William O. Douglas's case opinions on the postwar Supreme Court constituted a vast exposition of civil libertarianism. Like his previously cited economic decisions, they reflected the lasting influences of Louis Brandeis on his legal philosophy. [16] Douglas's opinions also illustrate the importance of experience as a critical leavening factor in his judicial thought, one that led him eventually to discard one approach toward civil libertarianism in favor of a more uncompromising one.

The overall thrust of Douglas's postwar decisions revealed his increasingly close cooperation with Justice Hugo Black in the development of the "preferred position" approach to questions involving First Amendment freedoms. The Douglas opinions also present his side of a sharp debate about the nature of the judicial process that marked his tenure on the Court. Moreover, all were written with his eye on both the immediate participants in the case and his belief in their educational value for a large audience.

The vast numbers of his case opinions make it difficult to adequately assess their significance. Fortunately, Vern Countryman of the Harvard Law School, a former law clerk for Douglas, has compiled and edited a collection of Douglas's key cases in *Douglas of the Supreme Court: A Selection of His Opinions* (1959). In it and subsequent revisions appearing in 1974 and 1977, covering all of Douglas's years on the Court, Countryman reprinted annotated excerpts from over one hundred of the justice's important decisions.[17]

As one of his reviewers noted, Countryman's approach has some definite limitations relating to his selectivity and the way Douglas's opinions are presented out of the full context of argumentation in which they occurred. To this initial criticism, another may be added: the excerpts tend to fall short of illustrating the wide breadth of knowledge and sources Douglas brought to his opinions that would have appeared if they had been presented in full.[18] There are also definite advantages to be gained by the general reader and nonlegal scholar from the Countryman approach. Because of Douglas's style and his habit of moving quickly to the heart of the constitutional issues confronting him in each case, it is easy to present the essential points of his decisions as Countryman does.

Thus, while Douglas's approach to decision-writing brought him much criticism on the grounds that his speed and brevity made him too careless about specifics and caused him to oversimplify the complex issues before him, his habit of avoiding prolix legal jargon in favor of clear English prose was significant. It gives the beleaguered general reader a far better chance of reading with understanding his opinions than those of many other judicial figures whose writing is both diffuse and dedicated to the abstractions and technical language that keep so much of American legal writing beyond the grasp of even highly motivated general readers. For this reason, Countryman's volumes are, despite their flaws, the best starting place to sample the important themes in Douglas's postwar civil libertarianism as he applied them in specific cases. The works represent an honest, though sympathetic, compilation of what the author regarded as Douglas's most representative opinions.

III   *Postwar Case Opinions: 1945–1955*

Douglas's case opinions during the early phases of the Cold War reflected his deeply felt concern about the threat to fundamental freedoms caused by overreaction to the Communist issue. As Countryman and others have noted, Douglas voted consistently to uphold the conviction of those committing hostile acts in wartime against the United States when such cases came to the Court after war.[19] Douglas reacted sharply, however, in cases involving government action against belief, expression, and association.[20] In those, Douglas's belief about the "preferred position" of the guarantees of the First Amendment came into play. When this belief combined with his narrow perception of what constituted "clear and present danger" and his hypersensitivity to the procedural protections of due process, the result was a flood of opinions, many of them in dissent, in the early postwar years against the excesses he saw in state and federal loyalty-security programs. These programs and the legislative investigations that burgeoned in response to the charges of such figures as Joseph McCarthy, Richard M. Nixon, Richard Velde, and William Jenner swept broadly into the realm of belief and conscience Douglas held so dear.[21] Federal prosecutions under the Smith Act of 1940, the anti-Communist provisions of the Taft-Hartley Act of 1947, and the McCarran Act of 1950 were reinforced by a renewal of state prosecutions under a bevy of old and new sedition laws. Collectively, these antisubversion laws created a classic case of overkill.

Douglas saw great danger to the democratic ideals of free discussion and freedom of conscience resulting from the mood of orthodoxy created by such legislation. He expressed dissatisfaction in a series of opinions in cases dealing with the security issue, many in dissent from the majority opinions of his fellow justices on the restraint-oriented Vinson Court. In these, he sharply condemned the gross violations of individual freedom, though he did so in a way that reflected both his continued use of and growing dissatisfaction with the balancing and "clear and present danger" doctrines.

One of Douglas's most effective and pungent attacks on the infamous aspects of the federal loyalty-security program was his dissent in *United States* v. *Nugent*.

The use of statements by informers who need not confront the person under investigation or accusation has such an infamous history that it should be rooted out from our procedure. A hearing at which these faceless people are allowed to present their whispered rumors and yet escape the test and torture of cross-examination is not a hearing in the Anglo-American sense. We should be done with the practice—whether the life of a man is at stake, or his reputation, or any matter touching upon his status or his rights.[22]

Here Douglas's skill at using what C. Herman Pritchett characterized as a "biting and scornful" attack is clearly illustrated.[23]

Similarly, Douglas showed his dislike of legislative committee investigations of alleged subversives in his dissent in *Tenney* v. *Brandhove*.[24] In that case, dealing with the liability of members of a California legislative committee, Douglas held that the members of the committee had departed from their proper area of interest and had denied a citizen his constitutional rights. He chastised the Court's majority for its exercise of judicial restraint in the face of a critical constitutional question. He believed that the doctrine of legislative immunity should not be used as a cover for witch hunts, that judicial power should be exercised to prevent that excess.

Douglas also dissented sharply when the Court upheld the application of security programs that threatened academic freedom as he was convinced it did in *Adler* v. *Board of Education*. The Court in that decision upheld New York's Feinberg Act, which permitted the State Board of Regents to deny employment to teachers who had been members of alleged subversive organizations. A particularly objectionable part of the law held that past membership would be preemptive evidence of present membership. Douglas saw the case differently. He agreed that the school system need not become a forum for propagating the Marxist creed, "But the guilt of the teacher should turn on overt acts."[25] Again, as in numerous decisions in the Cold War years, Douglas admitted the need for a balancing process, but one that construed the "clear and present danger" doctrine narrowly. That distinction left the entire realm of freedom of expression beyond the power of the state.

Douglas also wrote several strongly worded opinions in cases dealing with questions of First Amendment freedoms and Communist party membership. Defining the "clear and present danger" doctrines narrowly as a check on action rather than thought, he asserted that freedom of association was also guaranteed by the First Amendment. His classic statement of this view came in his dissent in *Dennis* v. *United States* in 1951.[26] In that case, a number of the national officers of the Communist party were convicted under the Smith Act of conspiring to advocate forcible overthrow of the government. In sustaining this conviction, the Court held that the "clear and present danger" standard was satisfied because the group was indoctrinating its members to strike when they felt circumstances would permit that action.[27]

Douglas was convinced that the conviction of the Communists was based on their intent rather than the seditious conduct the Smith Act was designed to restrict. Drawing an analogy between the conviction and the doctrine of constructive treason that had once flourished in British history as an excuse for punishing men for their thoughts, Douglas insisted that such an approach threatened the vital tradition of freedom of speech. As he said: "Free speech has occupied an exalted position because of the high service it has given our society. Its protection is essential to the very existence of a democracy."[28]

Douglas did admit that even speech lost its protective status when the correct application of the "clear and present danger" doctrine came into play: "When conditions are so critical that there will be no time to avoid the evil that the speech threatens, it is time to call a halt." He insisted, however, that the status of communism in America held no such danger: "But in America they are miserable merchants of unwanted ideas; their wares remain unsold. The fact that their ideas are abhorrent does not make them powerful."[29]

Douglas's dissent in the *Dennis* case was his best exposition of his definition of the "clear and present danger" doctrine as a restriction on overt action rather than thought. To him, the doctrine should be read to reinforce the protections of speech and association in the First Amendment. The manner in which the doctrine was applied in the *Dennis* case thoroughly alarmed Douglas. It proved that the balancing approach could be gravely misused by an antilibertarian Court.

Douglas's willingness to expand judicial protections for freedom of expression in areas not related to internal security was also evident in a series of cases involving different aspects of First Amendment freedoms. It was clearly evident, for example, in his majority opinion in a 1948 case, *Saia* v. *New York*, when the Court invalidated a city ordinance prohibiting the use of sound trucks to broadcast religious messages by Jehovah's Witnesses as a violation of the First Amendment. Douglas ruled the ordinance unconstitutional on its face as a prior restraint of free speech in an opinion that

revealed his attachment to the "preferred position" approach to
First Amendment freedoms. It also revealed his continued adherence to the necessity of balancing individual and community
interests. He did this by arguing that abuses of loudspeakers could
be controlled by the use of "narrowly drawn statutes" rather than
by giving a police officer blanket power to deny permits.[30]

Douglas's opinions in cases involving the First Amendment
"establishment of religion" clause in the late 1940s and early 1950s
also illustrated his adherence to the balancing approach. In 1952
Douglas wrote the majority opinion in the case that upheld released-
time religious training for public-school students where the instruction was carried out in religious buildings instead of in the public
schools. In upholding the plan, Douglas carefully distinguished it
from previous released-time plans by pointing out that it involved
". . . neither religious instruction in public school classrooms nor the
expenditure of public funds." Brushing aside the complaint that the
schools were involved in policing the program, Douglas held that
such an argument was too strained. In terms of experience and
tradition, Douglas admitted that the First Amendment, within the
scope of its prohibitions, was complete.

That fact, though, had to be balanced with another reality.

The First Amendment, however, does not say that in every and all respects
there shall be a separation of Church and State. Rather, it studiously defines
the manner, the specific ways, in which there shall be no concert or union
or dependency one on the other. That is the common sense of the matter.
Otherwise the state and religion would be aliens to each other—hostile,
suspicious, and even unfriendly.[31]

By making use of the technique of *argumentum ad horrendum,*
Douglas made his case for a moderate establishment clause based
on judicial discretion. The task was thus one of determining the
constitutional standard applicable to church-state relations. As he
put it: "The problem, like many problems in constitutional law, is
one of degree."[32] There are few clearer statements of the balancing
approach in his case opinions.

As in his off-the-bench writings, Douglas's case opinions strongly
supported the ideas of procedural fairness that had evolved from the
Fifth and Fourteenth Amendments. One example involving a
national-security issue illustrated the intensity of his devotion to
procedural guarantees. The case, *Rosenberg* v. *United States,* was

one whose significance is still hotly debated.[33] It dealt with the appeal of Julius and Ethel Rosenberg, who had been convicted and sentenced to death under the 1917 Espionage Act for passing atomic military secrets to the Soviet Union. The Supreme Court had twice refused to review the case on appeal and had also denied the application of a writ of habeas corpus for a stay of execution.[34]

On June 17, 1953, two days prior to the scheduled execution and after the Court had begun its 1953 summer recess, Douglas issued a stay of execution on the grounds that the Rosenbergs' attorneys had raised a substantive constitutional question when they cited a new point in a petition for relief. In it, as Countryman explained:

The Atomic Energy Act of 1946 made it a crime to transmit atomic information to other nations, but unlike the older Espionage Act, it authorized the death sentence only on recommendation of the jury (which had not considered the question of penalty in the Rosenbergs' case) and only if the offense was committed with intent to injure the United States (which was not charged in the indictment or considered by the jury in the Rosenbergs' case). The question was, therefore, whether the Rosenbergs, whose offense began before but continued after the effective date of the Atomic Energy Act, were entitled to the benefit of its more lenient penalty provisions.[35]

Douglas felt that their attorneys had raised a critical question. Could the death penalty be imposed without a jury recommendation for a crime, part of which took place after the Atomic Energy Act went into effect? When the full Court reconvened, its majority vacated Douglas's stay, ruling that the Atomic Energy Act did not replace or inhibit the scope of the Espionage Act.

Douglas defended his granting of the stay in a strong dissent based on his perception of the procedural grounds applicable in the case. Insisting that there could be no death penalty without a jury recommendation, he argued:

Some say, however, that since *a part* of the Rosenbergs' crime was committed under the old law, the penalties of the old law apply. But it is law too elemental for citation of authority that where two penal statutes may apply—one carrying death, the other imprisonment—the court has no choice but to impose the less harsh sentence.[36]

He also attacked those who said the Rosenbergs had failed to raise that point in their earlier appeals, saying: "But the question of an unlawful sentence is never barred. No man or woman should go to death under an unlawful sentence merely because his lawyer failed to raise the point."[37] To Douglas, the Rosenbergs were thus victims of a critical denial of their procedural rights.

Douglas concluded by defending his grant of the stay in unequivocal terms: "Before the present argument I knew only that the question was serious and substantial. Now I am sure of the answer. I know deep in my heart that I am right on the law. Knowing that, my duty is clear."[38] After a final appeal for executive clemency was denied, the Rosenbergs were executed. Though Douglas was bitterly disappointed about the outcome of the *Rosenberg* case, it reinforced his belief in the critical importance of procedural due process, which was particularly important in his approach to criminal law. The position he took in *Rosenberg* and such criminal cases as *Haley* v. *Ohio* foreshadowed the leading role he would play in the expansion of the procedural protections for criminal defendants in the Warren Court years.[39]

CHAPTER 6

Civil Liberties: The Absolutist Approach

THE preoccupation with civil liberties that had marked the first decade of Douglas's postwar legal writing also dominated the last decades of his public career. Though his doctrinal approach underwent a significant transition, his goal remained the same: the fullest possible exercise of personal freedom for all Americans. Douglas's legal writing proves that he regarded its accomplishment as one of the greatest challenges confronting Americans.

I   Off-the-Bench Legal Writings: Mid-1950s–1968

Douglas's most comprehensive statement of his civil-libertarian philosophy appeared in his 1958 volume, *The Right of the People*.[1] The work was an expanded version of three lectures that he presented at Franklin and Marshall College during the spring of 1957. Utilizing what one reviewer called his "gift of patient explanation," Douglas presented a classic defense of the civil libertarian position.[2] Taking as its main theme the critical and ever-present question about the limits of freedom and authority in American society, he argued the case for personal freedom under three general topics: freedom of expression, the right to be left alone, and the civilian authority. The work is particularly significant because it indicates that Douglas's movement toward First Amendment absolutism was nearly complete by 1957.

Nowhere is Douglas's acceptance of that doctrine more apparent than in the portion of the book where he deals with freedom of expression. Drawing a sharp contrast between the lack of civil liberties in totalitarian states and their plenitude in democracies, he proceeded to extol the virtues and responsibilities associated with the right to criticize the existing order of things. The broad conception of freedom of expression that Douglas advocated was a shield against the conformity he feared would make us no different from our totalitarian enemies.[3] Warnings about the dangers of conformity remained a persistent theme in his work.

Douglas was not blind, however, to the complexities surrounding the task of turning First Amendment theory into practice, particularly when it seemed to threaten other community values. In his treatment of case law in this area, he criticized his fellow Supreme Court justices for restricting the scope of First Amendment freedoms.[4] He was particularly adamant in his insistence that the Court's obscenity decision in *Roth* v. *United States* could not be squared with freedom of expression as defined in the First Amendment. To him, the First Amendment was not a suggestion of moderation but rather a statement of absolute freedoms. Not surprisingly, Douglas's approach to matters of censorship and prior restraint was governed by the same premises.[5] He was convinced that First Amendment freedoms had to be exercised to be preserved.

The second portion of the work underscores Douglas's belief in the importance of preserving the right of privacy for Americans. In it he chronicled the procedural and substantive guarantees in the Constitution that provided a basis for the judicial protection of that right. In reference to the specific rights associated with privacy, he stated that some of them were ". . . in the vague penumbra of the law because the final word has not yet been written."[6] The "penumbra" concept was later to become the basis of *Griswold* v. *Connecticut,* Douglas's most significant opinion on the right of privacy.[7]

He found much support for his view of privacy in the writings of his mentor, Louis Brandeis, who had spoken bluntly about the right to be left alone by the government as a comprehensive one.[8] Again returning to the contrast between totalitarian and democratic societies, Douglas emphasized that the crucial difference went beyond material things into the realm of the mind and spirit. He was certain that much of the liberty of Americans centered in the specific protections against government interference with this right.

Douglas's discussion of the freedom of conscience guaranteed by the First Amendment revealed the philosophy underlying his position in the later school-prayer and Bible-reading cases.[9] By emphasizing the idea of a neutral state, he viewed its religion clauses as a strong break from tradition designed to avoid the acrimony that sectarianism had caused in the colonial period. He described the right associated with freedom of conscience as a sweeping one, including within its scope all forms of conscientious objection.

In a discussion of the relationship between the right of privacy and the rights of the accused that foreshadowed his votes in a number of later opinions, Douglas decried the failure of America to live up to the ideal that all citizens were equal before the law.[10] His traditional sympathy for the poor, the ignorant, and the weak was especially evident in his discussion of the worth of human dignity. He expressed particular dissatisfaction about current police practices in a number of areas of criminal law in which he felt procedural due process was violated. As in other aspects of his writing, he did not hesitate to state openly his position or his disagreement with his fellow justices and others whom he regarded as prisoners of their passion for security and order.

The final part of *The Right of the People* was entitled "The Civilian Authority." There Douglas discussed the traditional American aversion to military dominance as a product of our historical experience. He emphasized those aspects of the American constitutional tradition that created civilian control of the military. After examining the judicial opinions relating to military trials of civilians and the internment of the Japanese-Americans during World War II, he cautioned against what he felt was a growing trend to rely too heavily on military decision-making.[11] The solution, Douglas said, was to turn public opinion against that trend.

The Right of the People is a seminal work on Douglas's civil-libertarian thought. It signifies the maturation of absolutism in his approach to First Amendment freedoms and clearly illustrates his growing concern about the forces threatening American liberties. It underscores his belief that the best response to them is more rather than less civil liberty. His integration of constitutional case discussions with references to American history and current literature provide a great deal of food for thought on the relationship between liberty and authority in the American constitutional system. Much of his subsequent writing on civil liberties was an amplification of the basic premises that he developed in *The Right of the People*.

Douglas continued his discussion of the importance of civil liberties and the rule of law in the first half of his 1963 volume, *The Anatomy of Liberty*. Published as one of the books in the Credo Perspectives Series, in which leaders in different fields of endeavor discussed their fundamental beliefs, the work was the outgrowth of a series of lectures Douglas had originally presented to the law students and faculty at the University of Baghdad. Douglas's belief in the critical place of civil liberties as the base of the pyramid culminating in a world system of law was readily apparent in the work. It provides an excellent view of the integration of Douglas's civil libertarianism with his belief in a system of world law.

Asserting that his travels had revealed a universal longing for justice among the peoples of the world, Douglas stated that it was his intention in the book to discuss the essential values that would lead to the creation of a just society where none had existed before. Such societies could contribute much to the stability necessary to create a world without war. Its two most important features would be fundamental individual liberties and the rule of law.

In a discussion of the sacredness of man's rights, the right of revolution, and the specific guarantees in the Bill of Rights, he briefly summarized the status of civil liberties in American life. He emphasized the continuing struggle involved in gaining and preserving liberties by citing numerous examples from the American experience, the most detailed of these being his assessment of the *Brown* v. *Board of Education of Topeka* decision.[12] He insisted that equal protection of the laws could create a sense of belonging for all members of society.

The Anatomy of Liberty is fundamentally optimistic in tone. It speaks with pride of the American constitutional achievement and the role that civil liberties should play in the creation of a peaceful world. Perhaps because of its original audience, it is by far the most gentle of Douglas's later works. The sense of crisis that marked so much of his later writing is missing.

II   Points of Rebellion: *The Closing Salvo*

In 1970 the embattled, aging justice examined the role of dissent in America in *Points of Rebellion*, his most controversial and universally criticized book.[13] The work was both an indictment and a call to action. It consisted of three related essays: the first discussed how Americans viewed dissent, the second analyzed the causes of the dissent, and the last presented Douglas's proposals for the restructuring of American society.

The first essay was built around a contrast between what Douglas thought were the rights guaranteed by the First Amendment and the way that many Americans viewed those who exercised them in dissent. Emphasizing that the First Amendment was a safety valve that allowed Americans freedom of conscience in support of their beliefs, he argued that such rights made the critical difference between democratic and totalitarian societies. Yet, despite these protections, he noted that the country was caught up in a mood of insecurity stimulated by both past and present international and local tensions. An unfortunate result of that mood was the rise of a demand for orthodoxy.

Douglas felt that the previously cited mood of conformity had aggravated the situation and strengthened the forces of dissent by cutting off a critical safety valve. It blocked consideration of the sense of diminished man that Douglas saw as the root of the current dissent. It was on this point that Douglas identified so strongly with the young activists of the 1960s. He was certain that they shared his passion for the free play of the human spirit. His devotion to humanism transcended the barrier of age.

Douglas used the second essay in *Points of Rebellion* to describe "The Legions of Dissent," the forces pushing American youth toward direct confrontation with the establishment, a term he defined very loosely to include the groups making the major political, social, and economic decisions in the society. Turning to the question of why modern dissent was more ominous than its earlier persistent manifestations in America, he pointed to the sense of futility caused by establishment control of the two major political parties and the growing domination of our individual lives exercised by vast bureaucracies. That sense of futility led Douglas to warn of the potential for violence in the situation. He reminded his readers that violence, though episodic, was deeply rooted in American history. Many misread this aspect of his work and accused him of condoning rather than predicting violence.[14]

The third part of *Points of Rebellion* was a blunt discussion of Douglas's proposed solutions to the major problems confronting Americans in 1970. He was convinced that the magnitude of the problems was such that their solutions would require a great restructuring of our society. Most immediate would be the problems of reallocating our resources and creating some means of controlling key administrative agencies.

Again cautioning about the potential for violence inherent in the current frustrating situation, Douglas insisted that the ultimate choice Americans faced was a police state or a society based on human needs. The way to avoid the former, he argued, was through ". . . a vast restructuring of our laws."[15] He thus fell back on a time-honored tenet of legal realism, the use of law as a means of adjustment to social change. Specifically, Douglas proposed reducing the Pentagon budget, providing legal services for the poor in civil suits, revising laws that discriminate against the poor, and holding public hearings on administrative agency decisions. He also urged continued substantial progress of blacks toward equality and the freeing of the universities from CIA and Pentagon control so they could open the dialogue between Americans.

Written in the midst of his growing alienation from the establishment and his growing affinity for the youth-oriented activism of the New Left, *Points of Rebellion* made Douglas the focal point of still another controversy. His critique was so sweeping and its tone was so bitter that even some of his traditional defenders were hard put to support him. James Reston, for example, called part of his indictment of the American establishment "damn silly." [16] A number of his traditional conservative critics made use of the time-honored technique of lifting words out of context when citing his discussion of the possibility of revolution, thus portraying Douglas as something of a Robespierre in judicial robes. [17]

Douglas's stance in *Points of Rebellion* symbolized his deepening pessimism about the future of American society at the end of the 1960s. The impact of American involvement in Vietnam, the repressive mood that he observed, and the election of Richard M. Nixon in 1968 all contributed to Douglas's sense of disillusionment. He was convinced that America had lost its sense of purpose, that it had failed to meet adequately the twin challenges of effective world leadership and the creation of a just society at home. His subsequent case opinions and off-the-bench writings indicate that he maintained his critical perception of the establishment and his sympathy for the political activism of the youth culture. They also illustrate the consistency of thought in Douglas's legal writings. [18]

III   *In Pursuit of Absolutism: Selected Case Opinions*

It is not the intent of this discussion to survey the entire range of Justice Douglas's participation in the "constitutional revolution" of the Warren Court or his attempt to preserve its results in subsequent years. Those who wish may trace out his role in a number of excellent works such as G. Theodore Mitau's *Decade of Decision: The Supreme Court and the Constitutional Revolution, 1954–1964* (1967) and Paul Murphy's *The Constitution in Crisis Times: 1918–1969*. Suffice it to say that Douglas supported the majority in virtually all of the key decisions that comprised what Archibald Cox described as "constitutional decision making as an instrument of reform."[19] Moreover, he continued to defend the goals of egalitarianism and an open society in numerous dissenting opinions on the more restraint-oriented Burger Court from 1968 to his retirement in 1975. The emphasis in the following discussion will be, instead, on Douglas's adoption of judicial absolutism in the closing decades of his career. As in the treatment of earlier aspects of his case opinions, emphasis will be on selected opinions that illustrate Douglas's uses of that doctrine. Particular attention will be paid to his growing conviction that personal liberties must be preserved at all costs.

As L. A. Powe, Jr., pointed out in his seminal article on the transitions in Douglas's judicial philosophy, the justice's dissent in the 1957 *Roth* v. *United States* decision marked a watershed in his movement toward First Amendment absolutism.[20] In dissenting, Douglas reversed his former view, stated in *Dennis* v. *United States*, that obscenity was outside the realm of expression protected by the First Amendment. He had since become convinced that obscenity, however it was defined, was part of that broad area of thought given absolute protection by the First Amendment. As he stated: "By these standards punishment is inflicted for thoughts provoked, not for overt acts nor antisocial conduct."[21] Douglas's concern for freedom of thought had broadened to include all forms of thought as opposed to overt action.

He attacked the logic and wisdom of the standards for defining obscenity created by the Court with a combination of wit, evidence, and skepticism. He cited a survey to prove that the kinds of sexual stimuli varied greatly from person to person. As he argued: ". . . the arousing of sexual thoughts and desires happens every day in normal life in dozens of ways."[22]

His perception of the scope of the First Amendment was far different from that of the Court's majority.

The First Amendment, its prohibition in terms absolute, was designed to preclude courts as well as legislatures from weighing the values of speech against silence. . . . I have the same confidence in the ability of our people to reject noxious literature as I have in their capacity to sort out the true from the false in theology, economics, politics, or any other field.[23]

Some would say, given the continuing furor over obscenity definitions, that Douglas trusted the judgment of the American people more than they trusted themselves.

Douglas's acceptance of First Amendment absolutism was also evident in his increasingly rigid interpretation of the amendment's "establishment of religion" clause. In striking contrast to his application of a balancing approach in his previously cited *Zorach* v. *Clauson* opinion, he now emphasized the need for absolute neutrality in church-state relations.[24] Douglas voted with the Court's majority in the cases invalidating school prayers and scripture readings in the public schools.[25] In the first of the two cases, *Engel* v. *Vitale*, Douglas stated that he had been wrong to vote as he had in previous church-state cases to allow state-supported busing for parochial schools.

Thus Douglas's broadened interpretation of government neutrality in church-state relations caused him to dissent sharply when the Court in *Board of Education* v. *Allen* upheld the constitutionality of state-purchased textbooks for parochial schools.[26] In justifying his dissent, he drew a sharp contrast between what the Court had approved in *Everson* v. *Board of Education* and what it had done in the present case.[27]

Whatever may be said of *Everson*, there is nothing ideological about a bus. . . . The textbook goes to the very heart of education in a parochial school. It is the chief, although not solitary, instrumentality for propagating a particular religious creed or faith. How can we possibly approve such state aid to a religion?[28]

The problem in the law, according to Douglas, lay in its requirement that the parochial school had the power to select the books desired. Such a situation would draw the school board into either submission to or conflict with religious authorities. Whatever way the situation evolved, Douglas was convinced it would violate the neutrality required by the establishment clause. Douglas's subsequent concurrence in a decision invalidating subsidies to parochial schoolteachers' salaries and his dissent against the Court's approval of federal aid for classroom construction for religious schools were on the same grounds expressed in the *Allen* case.[29]

The depth of Douglas's attachment to the absolutist view of individual freedoms in the face of government regulations can be seen in his opinion in *Griswold* v. *Connecticut*, the so-called birth-control information case. In *Griswold*, the Court had invalidated a Connecticut statute that made it illegal to use any drug, medicinal article, or instrument for birth-control purposes or to aid anyone

else in doing so. In writing the majority opinion, Douglas dealt with
the recently developed right of privacy, something he had recognized as early as his dissent in a 1952 decision.[30] Douglas, however,
went much further than he had previously to describe and justify
the constitutional right of privacy, the right to be left alone by the
government.

Citing a number of cases that illustrated how the state could not,
without violating the spirit of the First Amendment, contract the
spectrum of available knowledge, Douglas took a bold step toward
a further broadening of libertarian doctrine:

> The foregoing cases suggest that specific guarantees in the Bill of Rights
> have penumbras, formed by emanations from those guarantees that help
> give them life and substance. Various guarantees create zones of privacy.
> The right of association contained in the penumbra of the First Amendment
> is one, as we have seen.[31]

Such penumbras, of course, entitled Douglas to build constitutional
protections around individual privacy by extending the Bill of
Rights by implication to the whole range of human relationships
that an imaginative judge could relate to its existing protections.

Douglas did not, as some of his critics charged, depart from reality
when he adopted his absolutist approach to personal freedoms. This
was illustrated by his 1973 opinion in *Doe* v. *Bolton*, a case in which
the Supreme Court struck down a Georgia law restricting abortion
on the grounds that it violated the right of privacy guaranteed by
the Fourteenth Amendment's concept of liberty.[32] That right, the
Court held, included a woman's decision about whether or not to
terminate her pregnancy. In so doing, the Court had held that the
right was not absolute but subject to medical and legal restrictions.
The sharp division on the Court on that point presented Douglas
with an opportunity to enunciate what he considered absolute and
what he thought subject to restriction.

In his concurrence, he explained his definition of the liberties
granted Americans in the Fourteenth Amendment.

> *First is the autonomous control over the development and expression of*
> *one's intellect, interests, tastes, and personality.*
> These are rights protected by the First Amendment and, in my view,
> they are absolute, permitting of no exceptions.[33]

There were, however, other categories where Douglas defined the
protections as broad but not absolute. Some of these were:

. . . freedom of choice in the basic decisions of one's life respecting marriage, divorce, procreation, contraception, and the education and upbringing of children.

These rights, unlike those protected by the First Amendment, are subject to some control by the police power.[34]

It is thus apparent that Douglas was not totally absolutist in his approach to constitutional interpretation of civil liberties during his later years on the bench.

IV Some Later Dissents

The persistence of Douglas's fundamental beliefs is clearly visible in his outspoken dissents in his closing years on the Court. He remained true to his faith, though he again found himself surrounded by a restraint-oriented majority that was far more willing to accept restrictions on personal freedoms than he was. As his opinions in the two cases selected as examples here indicate, he still looked upon them as vehicles for educating the American public about the values of the basic guarantees in the Constitution.

His concern about the dangers of military surveillance of and record-keeping on civilians appeared in his dissent in *Laird* v. *Tatum*. In that case, the Court had dismissed damage suits of a number of individuals whom the Army had listed as anti–Vietnam War activists. The Court did this on the grounds that these individuals had not proved that the Army had taken any other action against them leading to direct injury. Douglas dissented strongly from this view in words that reflected his increasing pessimism about the state of American society.

He refuted those who said such Army activity was no cause for alarm.

But submissiveness is not our heritage. . . . The Constitution was designed to keep government off the backs of the people. . . . The Bill of Rights was designed to keep agents of government and official eavesdroppers away from assemblies of people.[35]

Douglas's writing illustrates his belief that a society using the techniques of totalitarianism to defend itself risked the genuine possibility of ending up like its enemy.

An example of another of his longstanding practices, his stout defense of traditional procedural guarantees, appeared in his dissent in *Johnson* v. *Louisiana*.[36] The majority in that decision held that criminal convictions in state jurisdictions did not require a unanimous jury vote. To Douglas, such an anomaly between the federal requirement for a unanimous jury and the state lack of one was highly disturbing.

He was convinced that two centuries of American history had been shunted aside, with the result that

> After today's decisions, a man's property may only be taken away by a unanimous jury vote, yet he can be stripped of his liberty by a lesser standard. How can that result be squared with the law of the land as expressed in the settled and traditional requirements of procedural due process?[37]

Douglas was convinced that the use of a nonunanimous jury diminished its reliability.

Fully aware of the mood of the times, Douglas still insisted that the procedural tradition should not be modified because that would lead to greater encroachments on fundamental liberties in the face of popular pressure for more law and order. As he said:

> Until the Constitution is rewritten, we have the present one to support and construe. It has served us well. We lifetime appointees, who sit here only by happenstance, are the last who should sit as a Committee of Revision on rights as basic as those involved in the present cases.[38]

Such were the major assumptions that guided Douglas's attempts to preserve both the written and unwritten procedural practices in our criminal law.

His dissent in *Johnson* v. *Louisiana,* coming as it did in the period of reaction to the Warren Court's sweeping defense of the rights of the accused, signified his continued devotion to the assumptions that shaped his earlier decisions. Like a rock, he stood unmoved by presidential and public pressure. He maintained his disdain for procedural shortcuts to the end of his career.

As illustrated by the foregoing examples, Douglas's case opinions were dominated by one major theme: his persistent advocacy of civil libertarianism. Though the interpretive formulas that he advocated underwent significant transitions during his time on the Supreme Court, his major goal of a just society characterized by a broad range of individual liberties remained constant. Both his case opinions and off-the-bench legal writings indicate that as he grew older he grew more impatient with those who did not grasp the critical importance of his vigorous defense of individual liberties.

CHAPTER 7

The Lasting Douglas

T HE significance of an individual's contribution to the American literary tradition is, like beauty, oftentimes in the eye of the beholder. This is especially true when assessing American reform writers. The function of their writing is a pragmatic one, the creation of support for the basic changes that they seek to achieve.

It would seem appropriate, then, that American reform writing be assessed from the perspective of what it was intended to accomplish rather than with criteria more aptly suited to other kinds of writings. I do not intend to suggest that traditional critical canons relating to style and literary quality be cast aside, but rather that they be applied with an awareness of significant aspects of the American reform tradition—such as the techniques of advocacy—in mind. With these thoughts as background, I offer the following summary remarks about the significance of William O. Douglas's writing.

I *Realistic Romanticism*

The emphasis of William O. Douglas's writing is such that he is clearly best considered as one of the social critics who have contributed to the American liberal reform tradition. Assessing Douglas's career at the time of his retirement, Abe Fortas said:

Throughout his life, Douglas has fiercely occupied high ground—the highest that life on this earth offers. He is, of course, an idealist; but, for him, ideals are not abstractions; they are objectives demanding present fulfillment.[1]

Douglas's work contains the unique form of tension found in much of American reform writing, a tension created by reformers' pessimistic and realistic discussions of things as they were contrasted to their idealistic hopes of what could be. Like Norman Thomas and Upton Sinclair before him, Douglas is a "romantic realist."[2]

His writing indicates, however, that he lost some of his optimism in later years in the face of experience. His early enthusiasm for the reforming potential of administrative government, for example, waned once it became apparent that its misuses created serious threats to civil liberties and wilderness preservation. A similar pattern occurred in his reaction to the Alliance for Progress.

Despite the enjoyment that can be derived from his travel-adventure and wilderness books, most of Douglas's writing is designed to make his readers uncomfortable and move them to action. As one critic has stated:

Those qualities which distinguished his legal decisions and his public speeches—what *Commonweal* has called his "eloquent and optimistic devotion to civil rights and the well-being of the common man"—have been carried over into his literary writings.[3]

His style is marked by its "disarming simplicity." As critic Oliver Prescott noted: "Its quality lies in the character of its author, the warmth, friendliness, humanity, and bedrock idealism."[4] If readability is a criterion, Douglas ranks high among American reform writers and certainly close to the best in the American judicial tradition.

Any assessment of Douglas's reform writings must examine his efforts in three areas: law, conservation, and foreign affairs. His legal writing provides ample testimony for those who insist he was the most doctrinaire and committed civil libertarian ever to sit on the United States Supreme Court.[5] As the editor of the *Library Journal* put it: "The greatest tribute to him is in the writings of Justice Douglas himself—writings that represent a testimonial to the faith that a society can afford freedom, that people can rule themselves. . . ."[6] There is no doubt that Douglas left his fears far behind him.

It also reveals that his passion for justice was the predominant influence shaping his case opinions and off-the-bench writings. On the one hand, his preoccupation with this goal made him far less attentive to technical details and complex argumentation than many members of the legal profession and a number of scholars would have preferred. As Charles Ares, Douglas's former law clerk, admitted: "His impatience with dressing up his opinions with careful arguments will probably cause Douglas not to be ranked right at the top by the experts."[7] On the other hand, his preoccupation also had a more positive effect. As the editor of *Trial* said: "His opinions were often written so that even a lay person could read them; he kept them devoid of legal jargon and analysis."[8] Douglas's writing thus reveals that his approach to legal problems was result-oriented and that he was neither the greatest technician nor the greatest intellect to sit on the Court.

It also illustrates, however, something far more important about his reform activities. As the editor of the *Nation* put it in 1973:

> His great merit is that, as a vigorous judicial activist, he has specialized over the years in the defense of the Bill of Rights, whose provisions are under recurrent attack because they always conflict with the special interests of the moment.[9]

His writing illustrates his in-context development and application of liberal judicial activism on behalf of civil liberties and his continuing search for doctrinal means that would better justify their defense.

That writing also illustrates Douglas's involvement on one side of a continuing, bitter argument about the uses of judicial power. His judicial activism on behalf of civil liberties drew sharp retorts from a number of his brethren on the Court and neoconservative legal scholars who insisted on the exercise of judicial restraint and deference to legislative power.[10] As in the face of numerous impeachment efforts against him, Douglas stood firm as a rock in the defense of his beliefs.[11] His participation on the activist side of the debate underscores the consistent connection of his personality and legal philosophy.

There is a second area where Douglas's writing has had an impressive, albeit controversial, effect. This is in the realm of wilderness preservation, conservation, and ecology. Discussing Douglas's impact on these topics, California Supreme Court Justice Stanley Mosk commented:

> But to those who in recent years have become alert both to the wonders of unsullied nature and to the imminent dangers to our environment, William O. Douglas—the man and the judge—holds special admiration. His is the voice heard above the din of bulldozers and jackhammers; his are the literary portraits of forests and streams and beaches that loom infinitely more attractive than blueprints of subdivisions and refineries and canyons of concrete.[12]

His impact in this area came in large degree from the effectiveness of his writing because of its close ties to his experience. As Mosk put it: "Few contemporary scholars can express their love of nature—and fear of its desecration—as ingenuously as Bill Douglas."[13] He used his formidable descriptive powers in combination with personal anecdotes to extol the beauties and the cathartic effects of nature on man in the midst of a continuing contrast between nature's wonders and the dangers of its desecration.

Taking up the land-use ethic advocated by Aldo Leopold, Douglas carried it to what he felt was its logical conclusion. He argued that legal rights should be granted to the inanimate objects of nature.[14] His advocacy of this position made him a hero in the eyes of conservationists and the object of hoots of derision from those whose priorities did not include the protection of environment.

Douglas's writing reveals that his commitment to the defense of wilderness values was as absolutist as his later defense of civil liberties. Nowhere is the connection between Douglas's experience and his writing closer than in his treatment of the outdoors. His love of wilderness dominates this aspect of his writing.

The third important area of Douglas's reform writing, his discussion of America's role in world affairs and its relation to the search for world peace, was also organized around a challenge motif. His writing clearly records his rejection of the containment–status-quo political approach to American foreign policy in favor of one based on peaceful, economic competition with the Soviet Union and a "bit by bit" construction of a system of world law. Summarizing Douglas's efforts in this field, Abe Fortas said: "As a world traveler and writer, he formulated a vivid conception of a world inhabited by people of different customs and institutions, whose common objectives and entitlements he vigorously championed."[15] Writing from the perspective gained from his personal observation of many parts of the underdeveloped world in his travels, Douglas issued warnings about coming revolutions generated by nationalism, poverty, and exploitation that the United States would have to contend with far in advance of many of our so-called experts on the Third World.

Douglas's writings on world affairs offer a clear picture of the postwar liberal critique of official American foreign policy from the standpoint of a committed internationalist. It also illustrates how his internationalist perspective developed from the interaction of his personal observations with his faith in the rule of law and his growing concern about the dangers of nuclear holocaust. The considerable amount of pessimism he expressed in his later writings on American involvement in world affairs underscores the frustration he experienced over America's inability to alter policies he regarded as both unrealistic and dangerous.

II   *Activism and Its Critics*

Though he was never a stranger to controversy, Douglas's increasingly outspoken postwar exposition of his basic beliefs on and off the Court about civil liberties, ecology, and foreign policy precipitated criticism from a number of sources. This criticism provides valuable insights about the kinds of reaction generated by reform ideas. The reaction to Douglas's writing clearly illustrates the complicating effects that partisanship creates for those seeking an objective critical perspective on reform writers.

Douglas's remarkable ability to work rapidly through the case materials connected with his judicial responsibilities caused his critics to question the thoroughness of his work and the sincerity of his devotion to his position on the Court.[16] Regarding the question of the Court's workload, Douglas wrote near the end of his career: "In spite of the mounting load of work in processing, as distinguished from deciding cases, there is still time for research, deliberation, debate, meditation—and thinking, which is good for judges as well as others."[17] Such remarks caused a great deal of anguish among those who have argued in recent years that means should be found to reduce the Court's workload.

Additional ammunition for his critics came from his frequent globetrotting to remote parts of the world and his adventurous treks through various parts of the American wilderness. The numerous articles and books he wrote about these experiences provided justification for the charge that he was neglecting his judicial responsibilities. Douglas, in an interview in 1953, stated that legal writing came much harder for him than his travel-adventure writing because of the tough technical issues he confronted on the Court.[18] The brevity and conciseness of his case opinions and his off-the-bench writings caused others to charge that he tended to oversimplify the issues he discussed.[19]

Some of his critics, both on and off the Court, charged that Douglas lacked a proper judicial attitude because he threw aside the time-honored notion of restraint and dignified silence on public issues in favor of judicial activism and an outspoken stance on them. A number of these critics went so far as to charge that his strong beliefs and public advocacy prejudiced his attitude toward cases that came before him on the Court.[20] Douglas has explained that his determination to speak out on public issues came about as a result of his involvement in a case that came to the Supreme Court shortly after he joined it. The case, *O'Malley* v. *Woodrough*, dealt with the constitutionality of taxing judges' incomes. When the Court decided such taxes were constitutional, he determined that judges also had the right of full citizenship.

It should also be noted that there is a long tradition of judicial involvement in politics and public affairs in American history extending as far back as Supreme Court Justices John Jay and John Marshall. Justice Felix Frankfurter, who sharply criticized Douglas for his lack of judicial restraint, was a political manipulator par excellence. He, as many of his colleagues and historians have noted, was active politically on and off the Court.[21] The crucial difference was that Douglas refused to conduct himself in such a way as to avoid public attention. This behavior made him vulnerable to the charge that he had violated the unwritten and partly mythological canon that his behavior diminished the dignity of the Court.

None of this criticism, whether from partisan or scholarly sources, had any appreciable effect on Douglas. His writing, much of it an extension of his speeches, often led to howls of outrage from those who disagreed with his forthrightness. Several times, as when he called in 1951 for the admission of Red China to the United Nations and again in 1970 because of his involvement with the Parvin Foundation when conservatives called for his impeachment, Douglas chose not to respond directly to his critics.

When Eric Sevareid asked Douglas to respond to the charge that many of his opinions were marked by haste and failure to pay enough attention to precedents, Douglas answered bluntly: "That means they don't like my decisions." In response to the charge that he was too politically- and sociologically-oriented, Douglas argued that the judges of the past did not face such modern threats to personal liberty as electronic surveillance. Therefore, he asked:

Why take their wisdom? That's why I once said, to the consternation of a group of lawyers, that I'd rather create a precedent than find one, because the creation of a precedent in terms of the modern setting means the adjustment of the Constitution to the needs of the time.[22]

Douglas did not lack confidence in his approach to law.

The entire subject of Douglas and his critics deserves additional research. It is complicated by political partisanship, the clash of Douglas with the advocates of judicial restraint, and, finally, the controversy surrounding the Supreme Court's civil liberties decisions in the post–World War II years.[23] Douglas's passion for active involvement in public issues was certainly a typical response given the nature of his temperament and personality. It was also the source of much of the controversy surrounding his career. Borrowing an expression from Justice Charles Evans Hughes, it was to a certain degree a "self-inflicted wound." It certainly strengthened the sense of challenge that was so crucial to the development of the techniques of advocacy in his writing.

There is no more fitting testimony to the persistence of this advocacy than his posthumously published volume, *The Court Years, 1939–1975: The Autobiography of William O. Douglas* (1980).[24] Though the work suffers from disjointed narrative and haphazard organization caused by the intense physical pain Douglas suffered while writing during his stroke-induced retirement, it is still very much in the tradition that marked his earlier off-the-bench writings. His assessments of presidents, fellow justices, and other prominent Americans are typically blunt, as is his discussion of the significant constitutional issues that he confronted while on the Court. His portrayal of the late Justice Hugo Black and himself as true strict-constructionist civil libertarians and his contrasting characterizations of the late Justice Felix Frankfurter and current Chief Justice Warren Burger as something less than great should not be dismissed as motivated by any meanness of spirit. They are an integral part of what proved to be Douglas's final attempt to justify the wisdom and vitality of his political liberalism, legal realism, and judicial activism.

Finally, there is no more fitting summation of the major goals of Douglas's reform writing than that expressed in the preface of his 1974 autobiography, *Go East, Young Man,* where he wrote:

I hope it may help them see in the perspective of the whole world the great and glorious tradition of liberty and freedom enshrined in our Constitution and Bill of Rights. I hope they will come to love the continent, the most beautiful one in the whole world. I hope that before it is too late they will develop a reverence for our rich soils, pure waters, rolling grass country, high mountains, and mysterious estuaries. I hope that they will put their arms around this part of the wondrous planet, love it, care for it, and treat it as they would a precious and delicate child.[25]

William O. Douglas's strong sense of concern lest Americans fail to respond bravely to the challenges confronting them dominated his writing and tied him securely to the realistic romanticism of the American liberal reform tradition.

Notes and References

Preface

1. Michael I. Sovern, "Mr. Justice Douglas," *Columbia Law Review* 74 (April 1974): 345.

Chapter One

1. George Creel, "The Young Man Went East," *Collier's*, May 9, 1936, pp. 9, 95; Marquis W. Childs, "Mr. Justice Douglas," *Reader's Digest*, June 1939, pp. 58–60; Richard L. Neuberger, "Much-Discussed 'Bill' Douglas," *New York Times Magazine*, April 19, 1942, pp. 10–11; Fred Rodell, "Bill Douglas, American," *American Mercury*, December 1945, pp. 656–65; Wesley McCune, *The Nine Young Men* (New York, 1947), pp. 116–27; Louis Nizer, *Between You and Me* (New York: Beechhurst Press, 1948), pp. 96–99; Anna Rothe, ed., *Current Biography, 1950* (New York: H. W. Wilson Co., 1951), pp. 125–28; John P. Frank, "William O. Douglas," in *The Justices of the United States Supreme Court, 1789–1969: Their Lives and Major Opinions*, ed. Leon Friedman and Fred L. Israel (New York, 1969), pp. 2447–90; Milton Viorst, *Hustlers and Heroes: An American Political Panorama* (New York, 1971), pp. 344–65.

2. For a balanced critical review of the work, see John K. Hutchens's review, *New York Herald Tribune Book Review*, April 9, 1950, pp. 1, 15.

3. For a balanced critical review of the work, see Naomi Bliven's review, *New Yorker*, July 8, 1974, pp. 74, 78–79.

4. *Go East, Young Man*, p. 170; *Of Men and Mountains*, pp. 327–29.

5. *Go East, Young Man*, pp. xi, 3–115.

6. Ibid., p. xi; James C. Duram, review of *Go East, Young Man*, *Historian* 40 (November 1977): 140–41.

7. *Go East, Young Man*, pp. 466–69; "CBS Reports" transcript of "Mr. Justice Douglas" (September 6, 1972), p. 6; *O'Malley* v. *Woodrough*, 307 U.S. 277 (1939).

8. *Go East, Young Man*, p. 182.

9. Ibid., p. 170.

10. Ibid., pp. 441–53.

11. Ibid., pp. 324–30.

12. The best description of the development of his self-confidence appears in the first seven chapters in *Of Men and Mountains*.

13. Ibid., pp. 314–29.

14. "Toward Greater Vitality," *Today's Health*, May 1973, p. 54.

15. Ibid., p. 72; see, for example, his discussion of these themes in *Of Men and Mountains*, pp. 327–29; *The Right of the People* (Garden City, N.Y., 1958), pp. 57–140.

16. *Go East, Young Man*, pp. 55–86; Frank, p. 2450.

17. *Go East, Young Man*, pp. 76–78; Vern Countryman, ed., *The Douglas Opinions* (New York, 1977), p. ix.

18. *Points of Rebellion* (New York, 1970), pp. 54–55; *A Wilderness Bill of Rights* (Boston, Mass., 1965), passim.

19. *Go East, Young Man*, pp. 66–68; Frank, p. 2449. Douglas eventually met Borah and they became good friends. The Idaho senator played an influential role in bringing about Douglas's appointment to the Supreme Court.

20. "Underhill Moore," *Yale Law Journal* 59 (January 1950): 187–88; *Go East, Young Man*, pp. 127–62; Frank, p. 2450.

21. "Mr. Justice Douglas," *Columbia Law Review* 74 (April 1974): 351.

22. *Go East, Young Man*, pp. 57, 145–46, 160; Frank, p. 2451; Leon D. Epstein, "Economic Predilections of Justice Douglas," *Wisconsin Law Review* 1949 (May 1949): 533–36.

23. Thomas I. Emerson, "The First Amendment," *Columbia Law Review* 74 (April 1974): 353–57; "The Lasting Influence of Mr. Justice Brandeis," *Temple Law Quarterly* 19 (April 1946): 361–70; *Go East, Young Man*, pp. 441–49.

24. *Go East, Young Man*, pp. 350, 444; Louis Brandeis, *Other People's Money and How the Bankers Use It* (New York: Frederick A. Stokes Co., 1914); 208 U.S. 412 (1908).

25. Epstein, "Economic Predilections of Justice Douglas," p. 538; Richard L. Neuberger, "Mr. Justice Douglas," *Harper's Magazine*, August 1942, p. 317.

26. Frank, p. 2460.

27. For a balanced critical review of the work, see Joseph V. Kline's review, *Yale Law Journal* 41 (June 1932): 1255–58.

28. Review of *Student's Manual of Bankruptcy Law and Practice* by Lee E. Joslyn, *Illinois Law Review* 22 (November 1927): 347–48; see also review of *New York Law of Damages* by Briscoe Baldwin Clark, *Columbia Law Review* 26 (June 1926): 780–82; review of *Cases on the Law of Bankruptcy* by Evans Holbrook and Ralph W. Aigler, *Yale Law Journal* 37 (March 1928): 685–87; review of *Cases on the Law of Bankruptcy* by William Everett Britton, *Illinois Law Review* 24 (May 1929): 121–22.

29. Review of *Cases on Damages* by Joseph Henry Beale and *Cases on Damages* by Judson A. Crane, *Yale Law Journal* 38 (March 1929): 698.

30. Review of *Cases on the Law of Bankruptcy*, by William Everett Britton, p. 122.

31. Review of *Law and Practice of Receivers* by Ralph E. Clark, *Yale Law Journal* 39 (February 1930): 593.

32. "Vicarious Liability and Administration of Risk II," *Yale Law Journal* 38 (April 1929): 745.

33. (With Carrol M. Shanks) "Insulation from Liability through Subsidiary Corporations," *Yale Law Journal* 39 (December 1929): 218.

34. Arthur Stone Dewing, review of *Cases and Materials on the Law of Corporate Reorganization*, *Harvard Law Review* 45 (April 1932): 1138–39; *Cases and Materials on the Law of Corporate Reorganization*, p. iii.

35. Dewing, p. 1138.

36. (With William Clark and Dorothy S. Thomas) "The Business Failures Project—A Problem in Methodology," *Yale Law Journal* 39 (May 1930): 1013–24; (with Dorothy S. Thomas) "The Business Failures Project—II: An Analysis of Methods of Investigation," *Yale Law Journal* 40 (May 1931): 1034–54.

37. "The Business Failures Project—A Problem in Methodology," p. 1013.

38. Review of *The Law of Insolvency in British India* by Dinshah Fardunji Mulla, *Yale Law Journal* 40 (March 1931): 840.

39. *We the Judges: Studies in American and Indian Constitutional Law from Marshall to Mukherjea* (Garden City, N.Y., 1956).

40. *Harvard Law Review* 44 (May 1931): 1164–65.

41. Ibid., p. 1165; see also Frank, p. 2452.

42. "Some Functional Aspects of Bankruptcy," *Yale Law Journal* 41 (January 1932): 329–64; (with J. Howard Marshall) "A Factual Study of Bankruptcy Administration and Some Suggestions," *Columbia Law Review* 32 (January 1932): 25–59; "Wage Earner Bankruptcies—State vs. Federal Control," *Yale Law Journal* 42 (February 1933): 591–642; (with Jerome Frank) "Landlords' Claims in Reorganizations," *Yale Law Journal* 42 (May 1933): 1003–50.

43. "Wage Earner Bankruptcies—State vs. Federal Control," p. 642.

44. "Landlords' Claims in Reorganizations," pp. 1041–50.

45. "The Hastings Bill and Lessons Learned from the Bankruptcy Studies," *National Association of Referees in Bankruptcy* 7 (October 1932). Page references in text.

46. "Economic Predilections of Justice Douglas," p. 536.

47. Frank, p. 2452; Oral History Interview with William O. Douglas by John F. Stewart (November 9, 1967), pp. 1–3, John F. Kennedy Presidential Library (hereafter referred to as JFK Library).

48. William O. Douglas to Franklin D. Roosevelt (September 19, 1939, November 10, 1939, and November 15, 1939) and Franklin D. Roosevelt to William O. Douglas (September 28, 1939, November 11, 1939, and November 21, 1939), President's Secretary's File, Box 144, Franklin D. Roosevelt Presidential Library (hereafter referred to as FDR Library); *Go East, Young Man*, pp. 317–42.

49. Frank, p. 2457.

50. Review of *Shareholders' Money* by Horace B. Samuel, *Columbia Law Review* 34 (April 1934): 787–93.

51. "Protecting the Investor," *Yale Review* 23 (March 1934): 521–33; see also Epstein, "Economic Predilections of Justice Douglas," pp. 535–39.

52. Chester Tevis Lane interview transcript, Columbia Oral History Project (1951), pp. 152, 232, 287, 330, 336–37, 341, 343, 389, 398, 406, 411–14, 444, 493, 496, 498, 501, 506, 517, 575–76, 698, 712–14; "CBS Reports" transcript, pp. 2–3; *Go East, Young Man*, pp. 257–96; William O. Douglas to Henry Morganthau (n.d.), Morganthau Papers, Box 249, FDR Library; memorandum from William O. Douglas to Henry Morganthau (January 29, 1938), Morganthau Diary, Volume 113, pp. 7–8, FDR Library; William O. Douglas to Franklin D. Roosevelt (February 5, 1938), President's Secretary's File, Box 144, FDR Library; memorandum from William O. Douglas to Franklin D. Roosevelt (February 18, 1938), President's Secretary's File, Box 144, FDR Library.

53. Frank, p. 2452.

54. For a balanced critical review of the work, see Henry P. Jordan's review, *Living Age*, December 1940, pp. 388–90.

55. George T. Washington, *Yale Review* 30 (December 1940): 398–99.

56. *Democracy and Finance*, pp. 5–56, especially pp. 18–21.

57. Ibid.; see especially pp. 197–213 and 230–41 for his calls for a new legal ethic that emphasized the social responsibility of business.

58. Washington, p. 398.

59. *Go East, Young Man*, pp. 57, 166–69, 171, 262, 313–14, 383, 416, 423–25, 466; for a summation of Thurman Arnold's beliefs about economics, see *The Symbols of Government* (New Haven, Conn.: Yale University Press, 1937).

60. *Go East, Young Man*, pp. 297–315.

61. *Democracy and Finance*, p. 245; see also Epstein, "Economic Predilections of Justice Douglas," pp. 243–47.

62. *Democracy and Finance*, pp. 241-47.

63. Ibid., p. 253.

64. *Go East, Young Man*, p. 315.

65. Ibid., pp. 455–70; Frank, p. 2454; Franklin D. Roosevelt to William O. Douglas (August 4, 1939) and William O. Douglas to Franklin D. Roosevelt (April 14, 1939), Official File: Supreme Court Reorganization and Endorsements, Box 117, FDR Library; see also the extensive number of favorable letters supporting Douglas's appointment in Oscar Cox Papers, Box 9, FDR Library.

Chapter Two

1. William O. Douglas to Franklin D. Roosevelt (June 10, 1942), President's Secretary's File, Box 144, FDR Library.

2. For a balanced critical review of the work, see Gerald W. Johnson's

review, *New York Herald Tribune Weekly Book Review*, August 15, 1948, p. 5.

3. Johnson, p. 5. Speculation about Douglas as a vice-presidential candidate appeared in 1940 and 1944. There was support among some liberals to dump Truman and replace him with Douglas as a presidential candidate in 1948. When Truman was nominated in 1948, he offered the vice-presidential nomination to Douglas, who promptly declined. Despite the rumors and endorsements, Douglas's correspondence, memoranda, and personal interviews reveal that he was indifferent to such talk, regarding it as complimentary but never seriously considering running for public office. Memorandum from William O. Douglas to Franklin D. Roosevelt (July 2, 1940), p. 5, Harry Hopkins Papers, Box 120, FDR Library; telegram from Eleanor Roosevelt to William O. Douglas (n.d.) and William O. Douglas to Eleanor Roosevelt (July 31, 1948), Eleanor Roosevelt Papers, Box 3751, FDR Library; Oral History Interview with Judge Samuel I. Rosenman by Jerry N. Hess (October 15, 1968, and April 23, 1969), p. 18, Harry S Truman Presidential Library (hereafter referred to as HST Library); Oral History Interview with George E. Allen (May 15, 1969), p. 27, HST Library; William O. Douglas to Harry S Truman (July 31, 1948), President's Secretary's File, HST Library; James A. Wechsler, "Douglas: The Best Hope," *Nation* 167 (July 10, 1948): 34–36.

4. *Being an American*. Page references in text.

5. Douglas stated that he felt its appeal was similar to that of the Sermon on the Mount.

6. Paul L. Murphy, *The Constitution in Crisis Times: 1918–1969* (New York: Harper and Row, 1972), pp. 232–42.

7. Review of *Being an American*, *Commonweal*, August 20, 1948, p. 458.

8. See Douglas's dissents in *Laird* v. *Tatum*, 408 U.S. 1 (1972), and *Holtzman* v. *Schlesinger*, 414 U.S. 1304, 1316, 1321 (1973); "CBS Reports" transcript, p. 6.

9. Murphy, pp. 213–47; Alfred H. Kelly and Winfred A. Harbison, *The American Constitution: Its Origins and Development*, 5th ed. (New York: W. W. Norton & Co., 1976), pp. 777–82; C. Herman Pritchett, *The Roosevelt Court: A Study in Judicial Politics and Values*, 1937–1947 (New York: Macmillan Co., 1948), passim.

10. Pritchett, *The Roosevelt Court*, pp. 89–90.

11. Frank, pp. 2454–56.

12. Ibid.; Epstein, "Economic Predilections of Justice Douglas," p. 540.

13. Epstein, "Economic Predilections of Justice Douglas," pp. 539–40; *Oklahoma ex rel. Phillips* v. *Guy F. Atkinson Co.*, 312 U.S. 508 (1941); *Wickard* v. *Filburn*, 317 U.S. 111 (1942); *United States* v. *Darby*, 312 U.S. 100 (1941).

14. Epstein, "Economic Predilections of Justice Douglas," p. 556; 310 U.S. 150 (1940).

15. *United States* v. *Socony-Vacuum Oil Co.*, p. 221.

16. *United States* v. *South-Eastern Underwriters Assn.*, 322 U.S. 533 (1944); Pritchett, *The Roosevelt Court*, p. 64.

17. 334 U.S. 495 (1948), p. 534; Epstein, "Economic Predilections of Justice Douglas," pp. 559–60.

18. *United States* v. *Columbia Steel Co.*, p. 535.

19. *Bowles* v. *Willingham*, 321 U.S. 521 (1944); see also *Yakus* v. *United States*, 321 U.S. 441 (1944).

20. 321 U.S. 144, 156 (1944), p. 158; see also Epstein, "Economic Predilections of Justice Douglas," p. 546.

21. Epstein, "Economic Predilections of Justice Douglas," p. 541.

22. 318 U.S. 261 (1942), p. 284; see also *Pacific Coast Dairy, Inc.* v. *Department of Agriculture of California et al.*, 318 U.S. 285 (1942).

23. Murphy, p. 134.

24. Kelly and Harbison, pp. 492–94.

25. Frank, p. 2455.

26. 320 U.S. 591 (1944); *Federal Power Commission* v. *Natural Gas Pipeline Co.*, 315 U.S. 575 (1942).

27. *Federal Power Commission* v. *Hope Natural Gas Co.*, p. 602.

28. For a full discussion of some of the attempts to discredit Douglas in the public eye, see the Westbrook Pegler Papers, Box 31, passim, Herbert Hoover Presidential Library (hereafter referred to as HH Library).

29. Pritchett, *The Roosevelt Court*, pp. 177–78; Epstein, "Economic Predilections of Justice Douglas," pp. 552–56; Frank, p. 2452.

30. 316 U.S. 74 (1942); Pritchett, *The Roosevelt Court*, pp. 177–78.

31. *Gregg Cartage Co.* v. *United States*, p. 88.

32. *United States* v. *Carolina Freight Carriers Corp.*, 315 U.S. 475 (1942), pp. 488–89.

33. *McLean Trucking Co.* v. *United States*, 321 U.S. 67 (1944), pp. 94–95.

34. Epstein, "Economic Predilections of Justice Douglas," p. 562.

35. "CBS Reports" transcript, pp. 18–19.

36. Memorandum from William O. Douglas to Frank Murphy (n.d.), Murphy Papers, Box 62, Michigan Historical Collections, Bentley Historical Library, University of Michigan (hereafter referred to as MHC).

37. Frank, p. 2456.

38. Despite this inconsistency, Pritchett, *The Roosevelt Court*, p. 130, places Douglas with Justices Black, Murphy, and Rutledge in the civil-libertarian wing of the Court on the basis of their votes.

39. "Evolution to Absolutism: Justice Douglas and the First Amendment," *Columbia Law Review* 74 (April 1974): 373.

40. Ibid., pp. 371–411.

41. Ibid., p. 372; Pritchett, *The Roosevelt Court*, pp. 93–107; Kelly and Harbison, pp. 751–70; Murphy, pp. 170–212.

42. 303 U.S. 444 (1938); 307 U.S. 496 (1939).

43. 310 U.S. 88 (1940).

44. 315 U.S. 776–77 (1942); see also Powe, p. 376; Pritchett, *The Roosevelt Court*, p. 221.

45. 308 U.S. 147 (1939); 310 U.S. 296 (1940).

46. 310 U.S. 595 (1940).

47. 312 U.S. 569 (1941).

48. 319 U.S. 105 (1943), p. 108; see also Powe, p. 377.

49. *Murdock* v. *Pennsylvania*, p. 109; see also Pritchett. *The Roosevelt Court*, p. 98.

50. Powe, p. 378.

51. 321 U.S. 573 (1944).

52. 319 U.S. 644 (1943).

53. 321 U.S. 158 (1944).

54. Powe, pp. 380–84.

55. *National Broadcasting Co.* v. *United States*, 319 U.S. 190 (1943); Pritchett, *The Roosevelt Court*, p. 170; Powe, pp. 381–82.

56. 318 U.S. 236 (1943).

57. 322 U.S. 680 (1944).

58. 322 U.S. 78 (1944).

59. Pritchett, *The Roosevelt Court*, p. 101.

60. 320 U.S. 81 (1943).

61. 323 U.S. 214 (1944). For discussions of the complex issues involved in the Japanese cases, see Kelly and Harbison, pp. 786–91; Pritchett, *The Roosevelt Court*, pp. 121–22.

62. Murphy, pp. 239–40.

63. Alpheus T. Mason, *Harlan Fiske Stone: Pillar of the Law* (New York: Archon Books, 1956), p. 673.

64. *Korematsu* v. *United States*, p. 218.

65. Murphy, p. 240.

66. 323 U.S. 283 (1944).

67. Ibid., p. 302.

68. Pritchett, *The Roosevelt Court*, p. 187.

69. 327 U.S. 144 (1946).

70. Ibid., pp. 120, 122; see also memorandum from William O. Douglas to the Conference (December 14, 1945), Frank Murphy Papers, Box 66, MHC.

Chapter Three

1. Stanley Mosk, "William O. Douglas," *Ecology Law Quarterly* 5 (1976): 229–32; Peter Wild, "Defender of Nature in the Nation's Highest Court," *High Country News*, January 27, 1978, pp. 1, 4, 5.

2. *Of Men and Mountains*, pp. 109–23; *Go East, Young Man*, pp. 41–54.

3. See his "Why We Must Save the Allagash," *Field and Stream*, July 1963, pp. 24–29, 57, for an outstanding example of this technique.

4. See Douglas's discussion of Muir and Leopold's ideas in *Muir of the Mountains* (Boston, Mass., 1961), passim; *A Wilderness Bill of Rights*, pp. 31–32, 34–35, 37, 42–43, 98–100, 151.

5. *Of Men and Mountains*. Page references in text.

6. Oral History Interview with George E. Allen, p. 4.

7. Monroe Bush, review of *A Wilderness Bill of Rights*, *American Forests*, October 1965, p. 38.

8. "My Favorite Vacation Land," *American Magazine*, July 1952, pp. 38–41, 94–99; "Wilderness Trails of the Pacific Northwest," *Mademoiselle*, April 1955, pp. 140–41, 194–97; "Man's Inhumanity to Land," *American Forests*, May 1956, p. 9.

9. *My Wilderness: The Pacific West* (Garden City, N.Y., 1960), p. 168.

10. For a balanced critical review of the work, see Howard Zahniser's review, *New York Herald Tribune Book Review*, November 6, 1960, p. 3.

11. *My Wilderness: The Pacific West*, p. 88.

12. Ibid., p. 206.

13. Ibid., p. 165, see also pp. 189–90.

14. For a balanced critical review of the work, see Charles Poore's review, *New York Times*, October 26, 1961, p. 33.

15. For a balanced critical review of the work, see Raymond Holden's review, *New York Times Book Review*, May 14, 1961, pp. 12, 14 (Part 2).

16. *Muir of the Mountains*, pp. 178–79.

17. For a balanced critical review of the work, see Stewart L. Udall's review, *Natural History* 75 (Fall 1966): 6, 8.

18. *A Wilderness Bill of Rights*. Page references in text.

19. Douglas notes that his idea for this came from a paragraph in the preamble of the constitution of the American Camping Association. See Douglas's dissent in *Sierra Club* v. *Morton*, 405 U.S. 727 (1972), pp. 749, 752.

20. Aldo Leopold, *A Sand County Almanac: With Essays on Conservation from Round River* (New York: Ballantine Books, 1949 and 1953).

21. For a balanced critical review of the work, see Pete A. Gunter's review, *Living Wilderness*, Spring/Summer 1967, pp. 48–49. Douglas received much assistance from President Johnson and his friends in arranging the visits to Texas that became the basis of this book. Jack Valenti to Dale Malechek (June 4, 1965, and June 7, 1965), White House Central File: Name File, Lyndon B. Johnson Presidential Library (hereafter referred to as LBJ Library); William O. Douglas to Lyndon B. Johnson (March 7, 1966), "Famous Names" Collection, LBJ Library.

22. *Choice*, March 1968, pp. 77–78.

23. *Farewell to Texas*. Page references in text.

24. The biblical reference is to I Kings 21.

25. For a balanced critical review of the work, see *Audubon Magazine*, May 1973, pp. 91–92.

26. *The Three Hundred Year War*. Page references in text.

27. See also *Go East, Young Man*, p. xv.

Chapter Four

1. See, for example, *America Challenged* (Princeton, N.J., 1960); *Democracy's Manifesto* (Garden City, N.Y., 1962); "William O. Douglas," in *Minnesota Writers: A Collection of Autobiographical Stories by Minnesota Prose Writers*, ed. Carmen Nelson Richards (Minneapolis, Minn.: T. S. Denison & Co., 1961), pp. 119–20.

2. William O. Douglas to Franklin D. Roosevelt (June 10, 1942), President's Secretary's File, Box 144, FDR Library.

3. See the collection of his wartime speeches in *Being an American*; memorandum for the President (July 2, 1940), pp. 2–3, Harry Hopkins Papers, Box 120, FDR Library; William O. Douglas to Franklin D. Roosevelt (January 11, 1943), Official File: Supreme Court Reorganization and Endorsements, Box 119, FDR Library.

4. *Strange Lands and Friendly People* (New York, 1951); "Revolution Is Our Business," *Nation* 174 (May 31, 1952): 516–19; "Democracy Charts Its Course," *University of Florida Law Review* 1 (Summer 1948): 133–48; "Indo-China: A House Divided," *Reader's Digest*, March 1953, pp. 144–48; "French Are Facing Disaster Again in Morocco," *Look*, October 19, 1954, 33–37.

5. *Towards a Global Federalism* (New York 1968); "Peace Within Our Grasp," *Nation* 168 (April 30, 1949): 497–98; "Towards a Rule of Law in World Affairs," *Saturday Review*, March 11, 1961, pp. 19–21, 40–41.

6. *Being an American*. Page references in text.

7. The speech is reprinted as "Democracy Charts Its Course."

8. See, for example, *Strange Lands and Friendly People*, pp. 315–27; *Russian Journey*, pp. 228–44.

9. For a balanced critical review of the work, see Joseph G. Harrison's review, *Christian Science Monitor*, November 1, 1951, p. 13. Douglas's correspondence reveals that he shared his observations about his foreign journeys with President Harry S Truman. William O. Douglas to Harry S Truman (June 12, 1949, and October 19, 1950), President's Personal File, HST Library; William O. Douglas to Harry S Truman (August 23, 1951), President's Secretary's File, HST Library; Harry S Truman to William O. Douglas (June 16, 1950, and June 14, 1952), President's Personal File, HST Library; Harry S Truman to William O. Douglas (November 1, 1950), Official File, HST Library; Appointment Schedule (November 3, 1950), Matthew J. Connelly Files, HST Library.

10. *Strange Lands and Friendly People*. Page references in text.

11. See, for example, his discussion of the nature of civil rights in the Soviet system in *Russian Journey*, pp. 174–91. For a balanced critical review of this work, see Leslie C. Stevens's review, *Saturday Review*, June 9, 1956, p. 12.

12. *Russian Journey*. Page references in text.

13. For a balanced critical review of the work, see A. T. Steele's review, *New York Herald Tribune Book Review*, November 9, 1958, pp. 1, 12.

14. *Booklist* 55 (November 1, 1958): 112.

15. *West of the Indus*, p. 501.

16. Ibid., p. 502.

17. For a balanced critical review of the work, see Sidney J. Harris's review, *Saturday Review*, July 2, 1960, p. 21.

18. Eugene F. Kramer, review of *America Challenged*, *Christian Century*, August 17, 1960, p. 950.

19. *America Challenged*. Page references in text.

20. For a balanced critical review of the work, see *Kirkus* 30 (February 1, 1962): 151.

21. *Democracy's Manifesto*. Page references in text.

22. Douglas expanded his treatment of the role of the United Nations in the creation of world law and federalism in *The Anatomy of Liberty: The Rights of Man Without Force* (New York, 1963), pp. 106–78. His discussion in that work marked the high point of his optimism about the chances for a system of world law.

23. *The Rule of Law in World Affairs*, pp. 28–29.

24. For a balanced critical review of the work, see Roger Baldwin's review, *Saturday Review*, January 4, 1964, p. 79.

25. For examples of his continued advocacy of this approach, see William O. Douglas to Lyndon B. Johnson (March 27, 1964, and March 30, 1964), "Famous Names" Collection, LBJ Library.

26. For a balanced critical review of the work, see Eugene Holtman's review, *Library Journal* 93 (November 1, 1968): 4148–49.

27. *Towards a Global Federalism*, p. 163.

28. See also Douglas's opinion in *Holtzman* v. *Schlesinger* and his dissent in *Laird* v. *Tatum* for examples of his sympathy for those involved in antiwar activities during the Vietnam conflict.

29. *Towards a Global Federalism*, p. 165. As he makes clear on p. 166, he also sees the Communist world as caught up in the grip of racism.

30. Ibid., p. 167.

31. *International Dissent*, p. 8. For a balanced critical review of the work, see Alfred M. Bingham's review, *Saturday Review*, May 8, 1971, p. 30.

32. See "Douglas: A Different Kind of Judge," *U.S. News & World Report*, September 14, 1951, pp. 50, 52, 54–55, for a perspective on the storm raised by his early support of the recognition of Red China.

33. *International Dissent*, p. 147.

34. Ibid., p. 149.

35. Ibid., p. 153.

36. For a balanced critical review of the work, see Edward S. Milenky's review, *American Political Science Review* 68 (June 1974): 861–62.

37. *Holocaust or Hemispheric Co-op*, p. 207.

Chapter Five

1. *Record of the Association of the Bar of the City of New York* 4 (May 1949): 152–79.

2. Ibid., p. 152.

3. *Journal of the American Judicature Society* 31 (April 1948): 166–70.

4. Ibid., p. 167.

5. *New York Times Magazine*, January 13, 1952, p. 37.

6. "Too Many Short Cuts," *New Republic*, November 23, 1953, pp. 9–11.

7. "The Dissenting Opinion," *Lawyers Guild Review* 8 (November/December 1948): 469.

8. For a balanced critical review of this work, see Ralph H. Gabriel's review, *Saturday Review*, November 6, 1954, pp. 37, 48–49.

9. S. Stephenson Smith, review of *An Almanac of Liberty*, *Library Journal* 79 (November 15, 1954): 2210.

10. For a balanced critical review of the work, see Fred Rodell's review, *Saturday Review*, February 4, 1956, pp. 16–17. For a shortened version of this book, see "The Bill of Rights, Due Process, and Federalism in India," *Minnesota Law Review* 40 (December 1955): 1–40.

11. *We the Judges*, pp. 61–62; see also 328 U.S. 549 (1946); 339 U.S. 276 (1950).

12. *We the Judges*, p. 64.

13. Ibid., p. 147.

14. Ibid., p. 190.

15. Ibid., p. 441.

16. "The Lasting Influence of Mr. Justice Brandeis," pp. 361–70. Douglas also continued his application of Brandeisian economic policies in his postwar antitrust decisions. See, for example, *United States* v. *Columbia Steel Co.;* Epstein, "Economic Predilections of Justice Douglas," pp. 556–59.

17. *The Judicial Record of Justice William O. Douglas* (Cambridge, Mass., 1974); *The Douglas Opinions*.

18. Alexander M. Bickel, Jr., review of *Douglas of the Supreme Court*, *New Republic*, September 14, 1959, pp. 20–21.

19. *The Douglas Opinions*, p. 198; *Haupt* v. *United States*, 330 U.S. 631 (1947); *Kawakita* v. *United States*, 343 U.S. 717 (1952).

20. Leon D. Epstein, "Justice Douglas and Civil Liberties," *Wisconsin*

Law Review 1951 (January 1951): 156–57; Murphy, pp. 264–65; Kelly and Harbison, pp. 755, 759, 761.

21. Murphy, pp. 279–309; Kelly and Harbison, pp. 825–51.

22. 346 U.S. 1 (1953), p. 13; see also his dissent in *Bailey* v. *Richardson*, 341 U.S. 918 (1951).

23. *Civil Liberties and the Vinson Court* (Chicago: University of Chicago Press, 1954), p. 247.

24. 341 U.S. 367 (1951).

25. 342 U.S. 511 (1952).

26. 341 U.S. 494 (1951).

27. Kelly and Harbison, pp. 829–31.

28. *Dennis* v. *United States*, p. 584.

29. Ibid., pp. 585, 589.

30. 334 U.S. 558, 562 (1948).

31. *Zorach* v. *Clauson*, 343 U.S. 306, 308, 312 (1952).

32. Ibid., p. 314.

33. 346 U.S. 273 (1953); Michael E. Parrish, "Cold War Justice: The Supreme Court and the Rosenbergs," *American Historical Review* 82 (October 1977): 805–42.

34. *The Douglas Opinions*, pp. 311–12; Kelly and Harbison, p. 827.

35. *The Douglas Opinions*, p. 312.

36. *Rosenberg* v. *United States*, p. 312.

37. Ibid.

38. Ibid., p. 313.

39. 332 U.S. 596 (1948).

Chapter Six

1. For a balanced critical review of the work, see Edmond Cahn's review, *New York Times Book Review*, January 9, 1958, pp. 3, 29.

2. William M. Kunstler, *Saturday Review*, January 18, 1958, p. 14.

3. *The Right of the People*, pp. 9–10. See *America Challenged*, pp. 3–10, and *Freedom of the Mind* (Garden City, N.Y., 1962), for examples of Douglas's continuing concern about the threats posed by orthodoxy and conformity.

4. *The Right of the People*, pp. 21–41.

5. Ibid., pp. 41–50; 354 U.S. 476 (1957).

6. *The Right of the People*, p. 57.

7. 381 U.S. 479 (1965).

8. *The Right of the People*, p. 58; *Olmstead* v. *United States*, 227 U.S. 438 (1928), p. 478.

9. *The Right of the People*, p. 91; *Engel* v. *Vitale*, 370 U.S. 421 (1962); *School District of Abington Township* v. *Schempp*, 374 U.S. 203 (1963).

10. *The Right of the People*, pp. 95–102.

11. Ibid., pp. 140–43.

12. 347 U.S. 483 (1954). For an extended treatment of Douglas's belief in the importance of the egalitarian thrust of the modern civil rights revolution, see *Mr. Lincoln and the Negroes: The Long Road to Equality* (New York, 1963). For a balanced critical review of the work, see C. Vann Woodward's review, *New York Herald Tribune*, September 22, 1963, p. 4.

13. For a balanced critical review of the work, see Morris D. Forkosch's review, *Georgia Law Review* 4 (Summer 1970): 830–65.

14. For an example of this reaction, see "Mr. Douglas' Revolution," *National Review*, May 5, 1970, p. 481.

15. *Points of Rebellion*, p. 92.

16. *New York Times*, April 15, 1970.

17. "The Wit and Wisdom of Justice Douglas," *National Review*, February 24, 1970, p. 191; Julian E. Williams, *The Case Against Justice William O. Douglas* (Tulsa, Okla.: Christian Crusade Publications, 1970); Alan C. Brownfield, *Dossier on Douglas* (Washington, D.C.: New Majority Book Club, 1970).

18. "Foreword," *University of California at Los Angeles Law Review* 15 (September 1968): 1374–76; "The Press and First Amendment Rights," *Idaho Law Review* 7 (Spring 1970): 1–15; "Some Dicta on Discrimination," *Loyola University* [Los Angeles] *Law Review* 3 (April 1970): 207–16; "Harlan Fiske Stone Centennial Lecture: The Meaning of Due Process," *Columbia Journal of Law and Social Problems* 10 (Fall 1973): 1–14.

19. Archibald Cox, *The Warren Court: Constitutional Decision Making as an Instrument of Reform* (Cambridge, Mass.: Harvard University Press, 1968).

20. Powe, pp. 393–94.

21. *Roth* v. *United States*, p. 509.

22. Ibid.

23. Ibid., p. 514.

24. *Zorach* v. *Clauson*, p. 306.

25. See note 9 of this chapter. See his discussion of the reasons for absolute separation in *The Bible and the Schools* (Boston, Mass., 1966). For a balanced critical review of the work, see Donovan Richardson's review, *Christian Science Monitor*, March 26, 1966, p. 9.

26. 392 U.S. 236 (1968).

27. 330 U.S. 1 (1947).

28. *Board of Education* v. *Allen*, p. 257.

29. *Tilton* v. *Richardson*, 403 U.S. 672 (1971); *Lemon* v. *Kurtzman*, 411 U.S. 192 (1973).

30. *Public Utilities Commission* v. *Pollak*, 343 U.S. 451 (1952).

31. *Griswold* v. *Connecticut*, p. 484. Douglas also found such privacy penumbras in the Third, Fourth, Fifth, and Ninth Amendments.

32. 410 U.S. 179 (1973).

33. Ibid., p. 211.

34. Ibid.

35. *Laird* v. *Tatum*, p. 28.

36. 406 U.S. 356 (1972).

37. Ibid., p. 383.

38. Ibid., p. 394.

Chapter Seven

1. "William O. Douglas: An Appreciation," *Indiana Law Journal* 51 (Fall 1975): 3.

2. James C. Duram, *Norman Thomas* (New York: Twayne, 1974), Chapter 8, note 1.

3. Stanley Jasspon Kunitz, ed., *Twentieth Century Authors: First Supplement* (New York: H. W. Wilson Co., 1955), p. 285.

4. Ibid.

5. "The Court's Uncompromising Libertarian," *Time*, November 24, 1975, p. 69.

6. John Berry, "A Debt to William O. Douglas," *Library Journal* 100 (December 15, 1975): 2277.

7. "The Court's Uncompromising Libertarian," p. 69; see also Nathan Lewin, "Vacancy on the Court: William O. Douglas," *New Republic*, November 29, 1975, p. 8; "Justice Douglas," *Nation*, November 12, 1973, p. 485.

8. "Douglas the Pioneer Departs: Stevens the Pragmatist Arrives," *Trial* 12 (January 1976): 3.

9. "Justice Douglas," p. 485.

10. Wallace Mendelson, "Mr. Justice Douglas and Government by the Judiciary," *Journal of Politics* 38 (November 1976): 918–37; Sheldon Goldman, "In Defence of Justice: Some Thoughts on Reading Professor Mendelson's 'Mr. Justice Douglas and Government by the Judiciary,'" *Journal of Politics* 39 (February 1977): 148–65.

11. "Douglas the Pioneer Departs: Stevens the Pragmatist Arrives," p. 3.

12. Mosk, pp. 229–30.

13. Ibid., p. 230.

14. See Chapter 3, note 19.

15. Fortas, p. 4.

16. William Cohen, "Justice Douglas: A Law Clerk's View," *University of Chicago Law Review* 26 (Autumn 1958): 6–8; M. Nettleship to Westbrook Pegler (March 16, 1950, and October 29, 1952), Pegler Papers, Box 31, HH Library.

17. "Managing the Docket of the Supreme Court of the United States," *Record of the Association of the Bar of the City of New York* 25 (May 1970): 297.

18. "Off the Cuff," *New Yorker*, February 7, 1953, p. 22.

19. For examples of this charge, see review of *Holocaust or Hemispheric Co-op, Choice* 9 (April 1972): 280; Joseph A. Page, review of *Holocaust or*

Hemispheric Co-op, New York Times Book Review, November 28, 1971, p. 48.

20. "CBS Reports" transcript, p. 5; review of *We the Judges, United States Quarterly Book Review* 12 (June 1956): 204.

21. Joseph L. Rauh, review of *From the Diaries of Felix Frankfurter* by Joseph P. Lash, *New Republic,* September 13, 1975, pp. 26–27.

22. "CBS Reports" transcript, p. 13.

23. Some of the more scholarly treatments of Douglas's jurisprudence include Powe, pp. 371–411; David W. Louisell, "The Man and the Mountain: Douglas on Religious Freedom," *Yale Law Journal* 73 (May 1964): 975–98.

24. For a balanced critical review of the work, see Christopher Lehmann-Haupt's review, *Wichita Eagle-Beacon,* October 26, 1980, p. 5c.

25. *Go East, Young Man,* p. xv.

Selected Bibliography

PRIMARY SOURCES

1. Books

An Almanac of Liberty. Garden City, N.Y.: Doubleday and Company, 1954.

America Challenged. Princeton, N.J.: Princeton University Press, 1960.

The Anatomy of Liberty: The Rights of Man Without Force. New York: Trident Press, 1963.

Beyond the High Himalayas. Garden City, N.Y.: Doubleday and Company, 1952.

The Bible and the Schools. Boston, Mass.: Little, Brown and Company, 1966.

(With Carrol M. Shanks) *Cases and Materials on the Law of Corporate Reorganization*. St. Paul, Minn.: West Publishing Company, 1931.

The Court Years, 1939–1975: The Autobiography of William O. Douglas. New York: Random House, 1980.

Democracy's Manifesto. Garden City, N.Y.: Doubleday and Company, 1962.

Exploring the Himalaya. New York: Random House, 1958.

Farewell to Texas: A Vanishing Wilderness. New York: McGraw-Hill Book Company, 1967.

Freedom of the Mind. Garden City, N.Y.: Doubleday and Company, 1962.

Go East, Young Man: The Early Years. New York: Random House, 1974.

Holocaust or Hemispheric Co-op: Cross Currents in Latin America. New York: Random House, 1971.

International Dissent: Six Steps Toward World Peace. New York: Random House, 1971.

A Living Bill of Rights. Garden City, N.Y.: Doubleday and Company, 1961.

Mr. Lincoln and the Negroes: The Long Road to Equality. New York: Atheneum Publishers, 1963.

Muir of the Mountains. Boston, Mass.: Houghton Mifflin Company, 1961.

My Wilderness: East by Katahdin. Garden City, N.Y.: Doubleday and Company, 1961.

My Wilderness: The Pacific West. Garden City, N.Y.: Doubleday and Company, 1960.

North from Malaya: Adventure on Five Fronts. Garden City, N.Y.: Doubleday and Company, 1953.

Of Men and Mountains. New York: Harper and Brothers, 1950.

Points of Rebellion. New York: Random House, 1970.

The Right of the People. Garden City, N.Y.: Doubleday and Company, 1958.

Russian Journey. Garden City, N.Y.: Doubleday and Company, 1956.

Strange Lands and Friendly People. New York: Harper and Brothers, 1951.

The Three Hundred Year War: A Chronicle of Ecological Disaster. New York: Random House, 1972.

Towards a Global Federalism. New York: New York University Press, 1968.

West of the Indus. Garden City, N.Y.: Doubleday and Company, 1958.

We the Judges: Studies in American and Indian Constitutional Law from Marshall to Mukherjea. Garden City, N.Y.: Doubleday and Company, 1956.

A Wilderness Bill of Rights. Boston, Mass.: Little, Brown and Company, 1965.

2. Pamphlet

The Rule of Law in World Affairs. Santa Barbara, Calif.: Center for the Study of Democratic Institutions, 1961.

3. Edited Works

ALLEN, JAMES, ed. *Democracy and Finance: Addresses and Public Statements of William O. Douglas*. New Haven, Conn.: Yale University Press, 1940.

COUNTRYMAN, VERN, ed. *Douglas of the Supreme Court: A Selection of His Opinions*. Garden City, N.Y.: Doubleday and Company, 1959.

———. *The Douglas Opinions*. New York: Random House, 1977.

———. *The Judicial Record of Justice William O. Douglas*. Cambridge, Mass.: Harvard University Press, 1974.

WALSH, RICHARD J., ed. *Being an American*. New York: The John Day Company, 1948.

4. Articles

"The Bill of Rights, Due Process, and Federalism in India." *Minnesota Law Review* 40 (December 1955): 1–40.

"The Black Silence of Fear." *New York Times Magazine*, January 13, 1952, pp. 7, 37–38.

(With William Clark and Dorothy S. Thomas) "The Business Failures Project—A Problem in Methodology." *Yale Law Journal* 39 (May 1930): 1013–24.

(With Dorothy S. Thomas) "The Business Failures Project—II: An Analysis of Methods of Investigation." *Yale Law Journal* 40 (May 1931): 1034–54.

"Democracy Charts Its Course." *University of Florida Law Review* 1 (Summer 1948): 133–48.

"The Dissenting Opinion," *Lawyers Guild Review* 8 (November/December 1948): 467–69.

(With J. Howard Marshall) "A Factual Study of Bankruptcy Administration and Some Suggestions." *Columbia Law Review* 32 (January 1932): 25–59.

"Foreword." *University of California at Los Angeles Law Review* 15 (September 1968): 1374–76.

"French Are Facing Disaster Again in Morocco." *Look*, October 19, 1954, pp. 33–37.

"Harlan Fiske Stone Centennial Lecture: The Meaning of Due Process." *Columbia Journal of Law and Social Problems* 10 (Fall 1973): 1–14.

"The Hastings Bill and Lessons Learned from the Bankruptcy Studies." *National Association of Referees in Bankruptcy* 7 (October 1932): 25–28.

"Indo-China: A House Divided." *Reader's Digest*, March 1953, pp. 144–48.

(With Carrol M. Shanks) "Insulation from Liability through Subsidiary Corporations." *Yale Law Journal* 39 (December 1929): 193–218.

(With Jerome Frank) "Landlords' Claims in Reorganizations." *Yale Law Journal* 42 (May 1933): 1003–50.

"The Lasting Influence of Mr. Justice Brandeis." *Temple Law Quarterly* 19 (April 1946): 361–70.

"Managing the Docket of the Supreme Court of the United States." *Record of the Association of the Bar of the City of New York* 25 (May 1970): 279–98.

"Man's Inhumanity to Land." *American Forests*, May 1956, p. 9.

"My Favorite Vacation Land." *American Magazine*, July 1952, pp. 38–41, 94–99.

"Peace Within Our Grasp." *Nation* 168 (April 30, 1949): 497–98.

"The Press and First Amendment Rights." *Idaho Law Review* 7 (Spring 1970): 1–15.

"Procedural Safeguards in the Bill of Rights." *Journal of the American Judicature Society* 31 (April 1948): 166–70.

"Protecting the Investor." *Yale Review* 23 (March 1934): 521–33.

"Revolution Is Our Business." *Nation* 174 (May 31, 1952): 516–19.

"Some Dicta on Discrimination." *Loyola University* [Los Angeles] *Law Review* 3 (April 1970): 207–16.

"Some Functional Aspects of Bankruptcy." *Yale Law Journal* 41 (January 1932): 329–64.

"Stare Decisis." *Record of the Association of the Bar of the City of New York* 4 (May 1949): 152–79.

"Too Many Short Cuts." *New Republic*, November 23, 1953, pp. 9–11.
"Toward Greater Vitality." *Today's Health*, May 1973, pp. 54–57, 72.
"Towards a Rule of Law in World Affairs." *Saturday Review*, March 11, 1961, pp. 19–21, 40–41.
"Underhill Moore." *Yale Law Journal* 59 (January 1950): 187–88.
"Vicarious Liability and Administration of Risk II." *Yale Law Journal* 38 (April 1929): 720–45.
"Wage Earner Bankruptcies—State vs. Federal Control." *Yale Law Journal* 42 (February 1933): 591–642.
"Why We Must Save the Allagash." *Field and Stream*, July 1963, pp. 24–29, 57.
"Wilderness Trails of the Pacific Northwest." *Mademoiselle*, April 1955, pp. 140–41, 194–97.

5. Book Reviews

Cases on Damages by Joseph Henry Beale and *Cases on Damages* by Judson A. Crane. *Yale Law Journal* 38 (March 1929): 698–99.
Cases on the Law of Bankruptcy by Evans Holbrook and Ralph W. Aigler. *Yale Law Journal* 37 (March 1928): 685–87.
Cases on the Law of Bankruptcy by William Everett Britton. *Illinois Law Review* 24 (May 1929): 121–22.
Law and Practice of Receivers by Ralph E. Clark. *Yale Law Journal* 39 (February 1930): 592–93.
The Law of Insolvency in British India by Dinshah Fardunji Mulla. *Yale Law Journal* 40 (March 1931): 840.
The Lawful Pursuit of Gain by Max Radin. *Harvard Law Review* 44 (May 1931): 1164–65.
New York Law of Damages by Briscoe Baldwin Clark. *Columbia Law Review* 26 (June 1926): 780–82.
Shareholders' Money by Horace B. Samuel. *Columbia Law Review* 34 (April 1934): 787–93.
Student's Manual of Bankruptcy Law and Practice by Lee E. Joslyn. *Illinois Law Review* 22 (November 1927): 347–48.

6. Manuscript Materials

The William O. Douglas papers are in the Library of Congress, but they were still closed to researchers at the time of the completion of this book.
Significant Douglas correspondence, as well as other references to his activities, appear in the holdings of the Presidential Libraries of Herbert Hoover (Stanford, California), Franklin D. Roosevelt (Hyde Park, New York), Harry S Truman (Independence, Missouri), John F. Kennedy (Boston, Massachusetts), and Lyndon B. Johnson (Austin, Texas).
The papers of former United States Supreme Court Justice Frank Murphy,

located in the Michigan Historical Collections, Bentley Historical Library, University of Michigan, Ann Arbor, contain much valuable information about Douglas's early years on the Supreme Court.

The transcript of the Chester Tevis Lane interview is located in the Oral History Office, Butler Library, Columbia University, New York City. It reveals a great deal about Douglas's personality and his service on the Securities and Exchange Commission (SEC).

The "CBS Reports" transcript of "Mr. Justice Douglas," an interview taped on September 6, 1972, contains a typically frank discussion of the reasons for his judicial actions. It can be obtained from the Columbia Broadcasting System's News Department.

SECONDARY SOURCES

CREEL, GEORGE. "The Young Man Went East." *Collier's*, May 9, 1936, pp. 9, 95. Typical of a spate of early biographical sketches characterizing Douglas as a young man in a hurry to reach the top.

EPSTEIN, LEON. "Economic Predilections of Justice Douglas." *Wisconsin Law Review* 1949 (May 1949): 531–62. Key article on Douglas's economic beliefs and their application during his term on the SEC and his first decade on the Supreme Court.

FRANK, JOHN P. "William O. Douglas." In *The Justices of the United States Supreme Court, 1789–1969: Their Lives and Major Opinions*. Ed. Leon Friedman and Fred L. Israel. New York: Chelsea House Publishers, 1969, pp. 2447–90. Sympathetic, detailed biographical essay that emphasizes the connection between Douglas's experience and his behavior on the Court.

McCUNE, WESLEY. *The Nine Young Men*. New York: Harper and Brothers Publishers, 1947, pp. 116–27. Biographical sketch that illustrates Douglas's brilliance, dynamism, and uninhibited nature. Adequately summarizes his wartime proregulatory economic decisions and his mixed record on civil liberties.

MOSK, STANLEY. "William O. Douglas." *Ecology Law Quarterly* 5 (1976): 229–32. Appropriate discussion of Douglas's significant contributions to the defense of wilderness preservation, conservation, and ecology.

NEUBERGER RICHARD L. "Much-Discussed 'Bill' Douglas." *New York Times Magazine*, April 19, 1942, pp. 10–11. Biographical sketch by a fellow westerner praising Douglas's sincerity and the importance of his western background and Brandeisian beliefs in his career.

POWE, L. A., JR. "Evolution to Absolutism: Justice Douglas and the First Amendment." *Columbia Law Review* 74 (April 1974): 371–411. The best analysis of causes and case opinions involved in the evolution of Douglas's civil libertarian philosophy from a balancing to an absolutist approach.

RODELL, FRED. "Bill Douglas, American." *American Mercury*, December

1945, pp. 656–65. One of a series of early postwar character sketches extolling Douglas as a potential presidential contender.

VIORST, MILTON. *Hustlers and Heroes: An American Political Panorama.* New York: Simon and Schuster, 1971, pp. 344–65. Well-researched, smoothly written character sketch that explains a number of facets of Douglas's complex character. Its emphasis on the lasting effects of early poverty and challenges on Douglas's adult personality is provocative.

WHITMAN, ALDEN. "Vigorous Defender of Rights." *New York Times,* January 20, 1980, pp. 1, 28. The most comprehensive of the many Douglas obituaries.

WILLIAMS, JULIAN E. *The Case Against Justice William O. Douglas.* Tulsa, Okla.: Christian Crusade Publications, 1970. Typical right-wing account that pictures Douglas as a radical, immoral Communist sympathizer who deserves impeachment.

Index

This index is limited to important items in the text, but also includes a selection of references to significant persons and subjects in the Notes. It does not include items in the Chronology. William O. Douglas's works are listed under his name.

156